Ultimate Dolly Parton Sticker Mosaic Art

LOGAN POWELL

DESIGN ORIGINALS
an Imprint of Fox Chapel Publishing
www.d-originals.com

TABLE OF CONTENTS

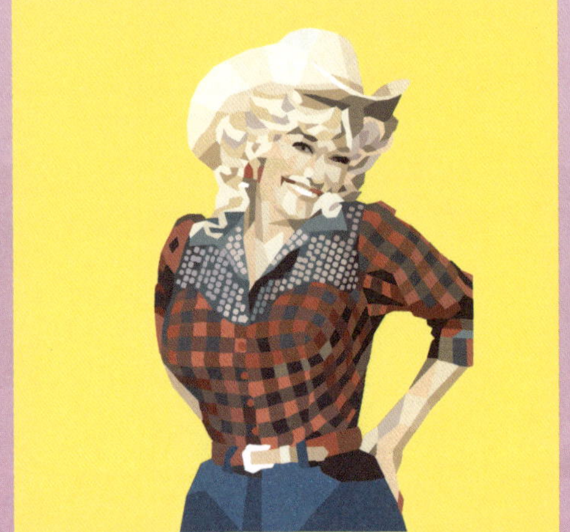

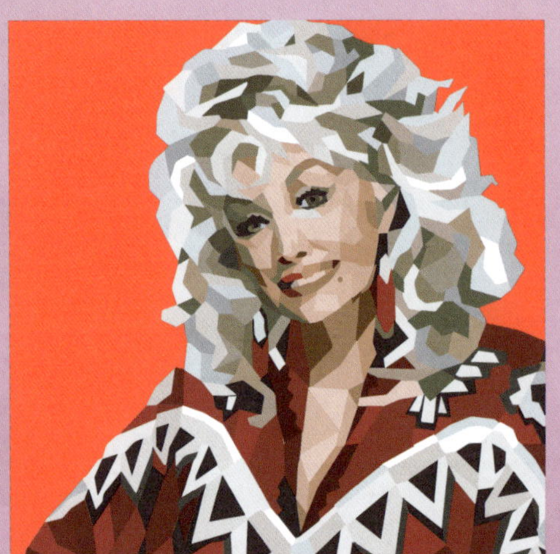

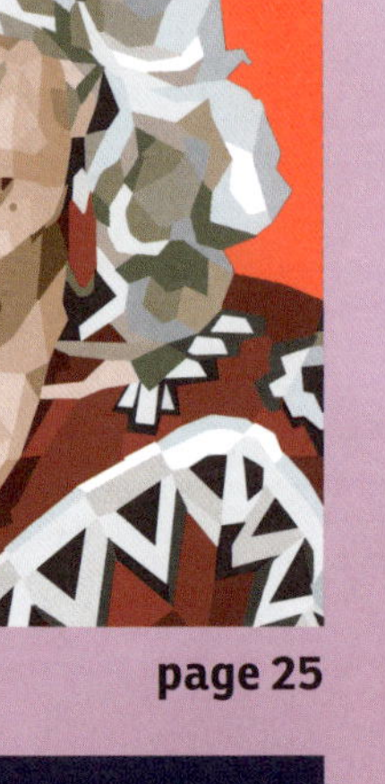

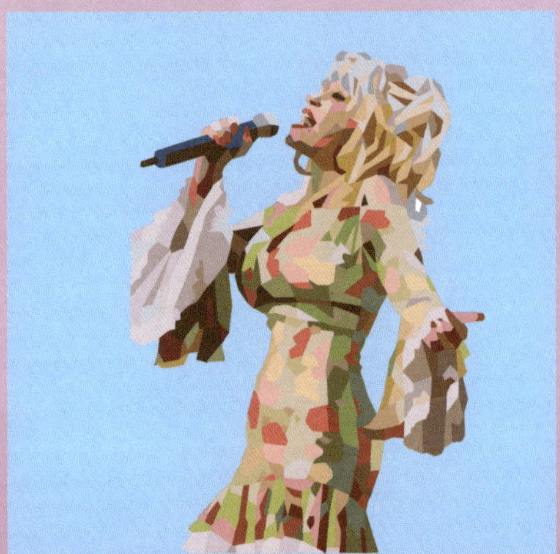

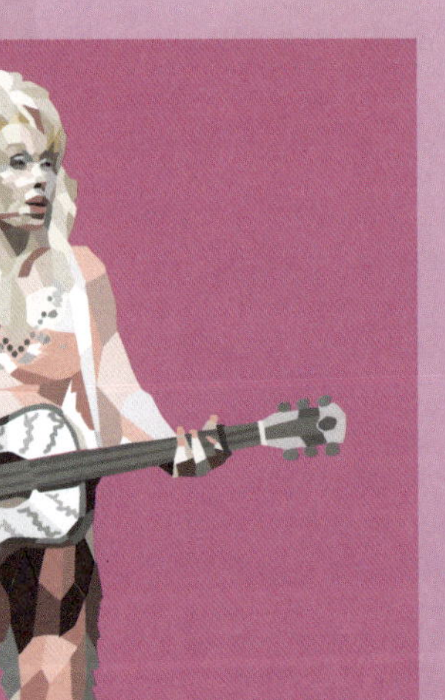

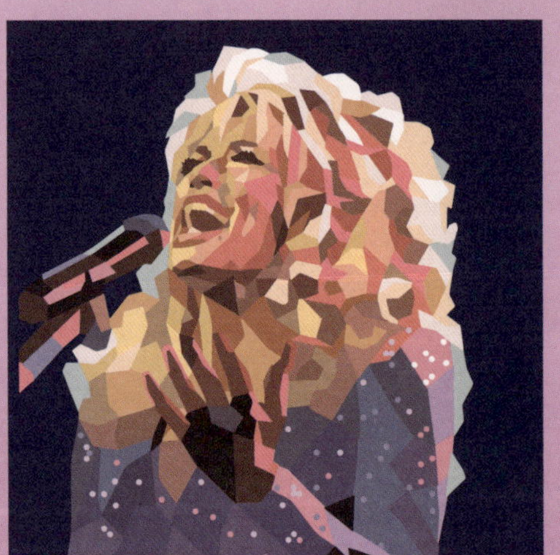

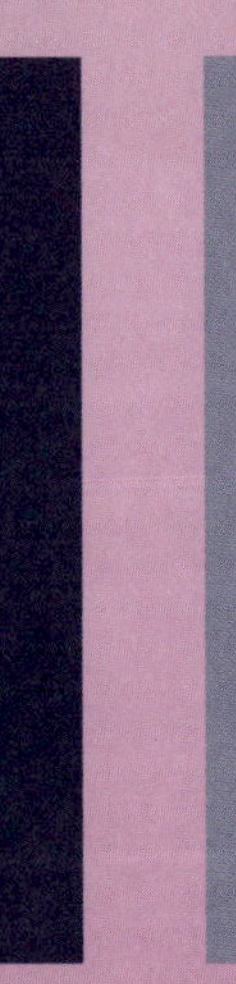

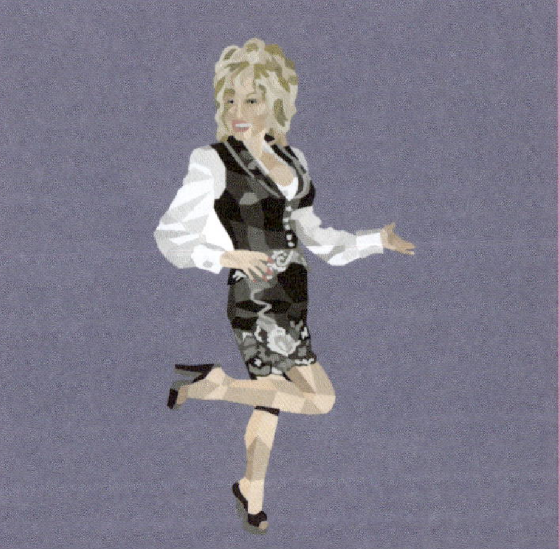

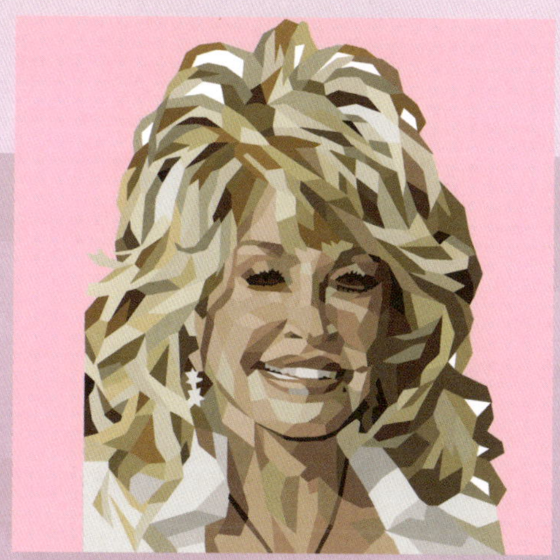

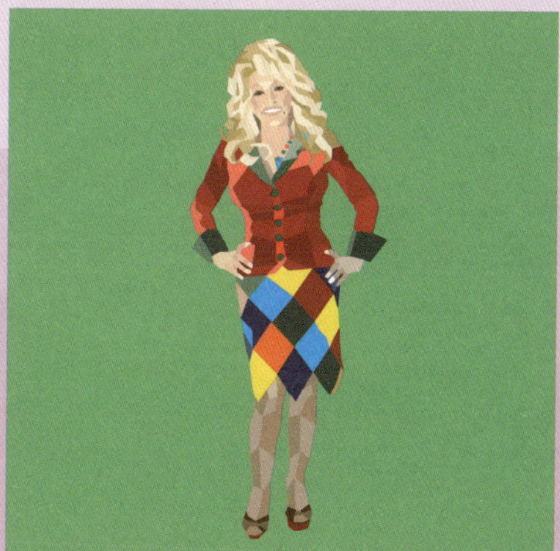

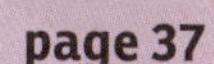

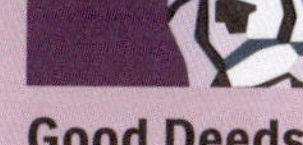

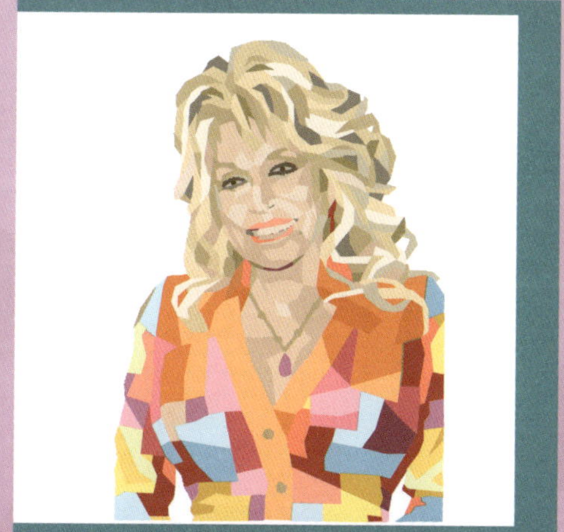

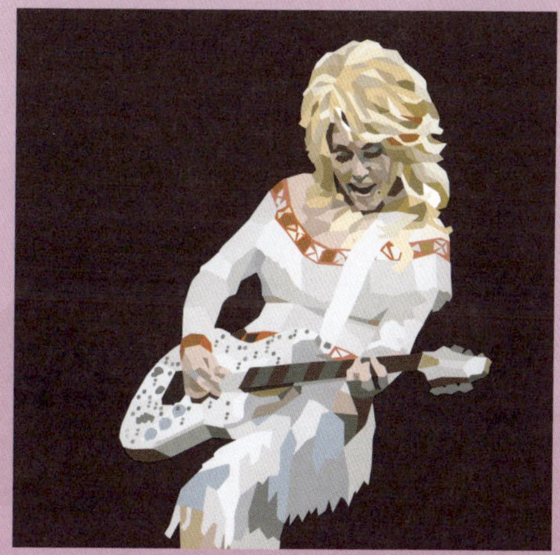

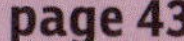

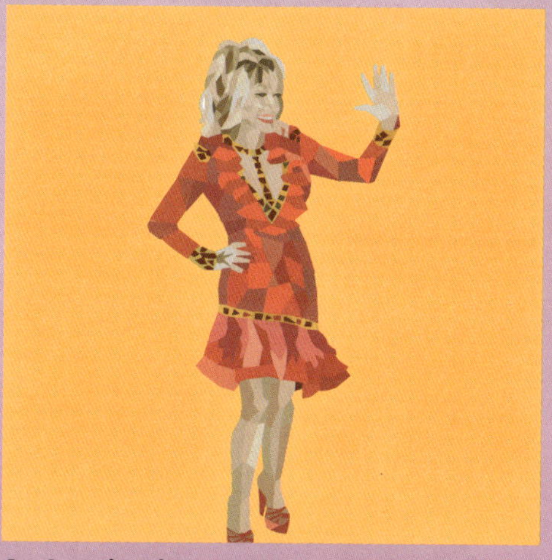

www.d-originals.com, an imprint of Fox Chapel Publishing,
800-457-9112, 903 Square Street, Mount Joy, PA 17552.

ISBN 978-1-4972-0718-9

Printed in China
First printing

Images used as inspiration for art from www.Shutterstock.com: Jack Fordyce (18 top, 29); Tinseltown (20 bottom, 35); Kathy Hutchins (21, 41, 45); Featureflash Photo Agency (18 bottom, 33), www.Alamy.com: Pictoral Press Ltd (16 top,17, 25, 31), AFF (20 top, 22, 37, 43), sandy young (27, 16 bottom), and www.Gettyimages.com: 20th Century Fox (18 left, 23); NBC (19, 39)

Additional Shutterstock.com images: Beatrice Mihaela (5 top), Tomas Marek (5 bottom); Storm Is Me (6 top).

Additional Alamy.com images: Pictoral Press Ltd. (7), MediaPunch Inc. (8), Album (10), Moviestore Collections Ltd. (11), The TN Collection (12), Emma Stoner (13).

Additional image: Jason Mecier, 6 bottom.

INTRODUCTION

Dolly Parton's impact on music, culture, and society is immeasurable. Her contributions to country music and her ability to cross genres have set her apart as a true musical icon. Beyond her artistic achievements, Dolly's philanthropic efforts have also made a lasting difference in the lives of countless individuals. Her Imagination Library® continues to promote literacy and education, and her donations to causes, like disaster relief and healthcare, have demonstrated her commitment to helping those in need. Dolly's generosity and compassion have earned her admiration and respect worldwide and have made her a true role model for people of all ages.

Dolly Parton embodies resilience, creativity, and empowerment. Her life story is a testament to the power of dreams and the importance of staying true to oneself. Dolly's enduring appeal and positive impact ensure that her legacy will continue to inspire and uplift for generations to come. In the world of music, Dolly's influence is evident in the many artists who cite her as an inspiration. Her ability to cross musical genres has paved the way for other artists to explore and blend different styles. From country to pop, bluegrass to gospel, Dolly's music resonates across generations and demographics. What better way to celebrate an icon like this than to create art, learn more about Dolly, and continue her legacy of kindness, strength, and determination for years to come?

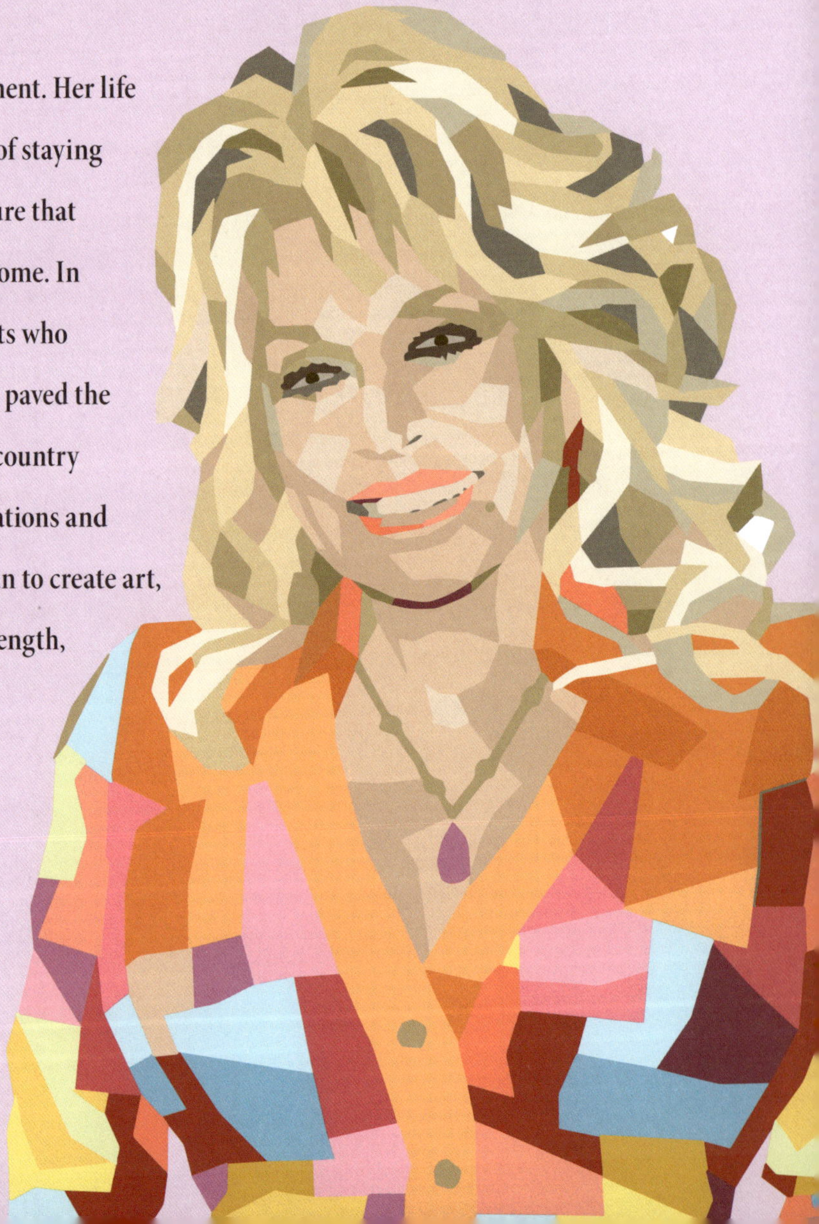

WHAT IS MOSAIC ART?

As you're working through this book to complete Dolly Parton–inspired artwork, you'll actually be working in a modified form of art that dates back to Greek and Roman times! Your creations made with paper stickers are a form of mosaic portrait making. And just like the legendary Dolly Parton, the Greeks and the Romans often created portraits of famous musicians! Read on to find out more.

Creating mosaic sticker art is fun and simple. All you have to do is match up the colored stickers to their corresponding number on the picture page. As you peel and stick, your design will slowly come to life, just like they did for the artists in ancient history! Mosaic is the ultimate way to create something big out of many little elements. Use your imagination; the options are limitless!

Something to think about as you create sticker mosaics of Dolly Parton in this book is the history of the ancient art form. Mosaic is an art form used all throughout history, dating all the way back to 3300 BCE. Mosaics are made by placing colorful pieces of glass, tile, stone, or even seashells together with plaster to create a larger picture or pattern. Mosaic art is like the world's oldest puzzle, found everywhere from Mesopotamia to the Roman Empire, even into the modern day!

Back in ancient Greece and Rome, mosaic art got so popular that it spread throughout the Roman Empire. Mosaic art was found in homes, palaces, cathedrals, mosques, and walkways.

Mosaic art depicted scenes, like a jigsaw puzzle, but it could also show beautiful patterns and shapes. Some of the scenes that were created showed scenes of animals, religious figures, politicians, everyday life, and nature. When the Renaissance came, artists chose to paint instead of using mosaic. But 300 years later, mosaic art came back!

Modern artists have fun creating mosaic art with many different types of mediums—some even make mosaic art with buttons or even different shades of toast! Now you can see mosaics everywhere, including kitchens, gardens, sculptures, park benches, and craft projects.

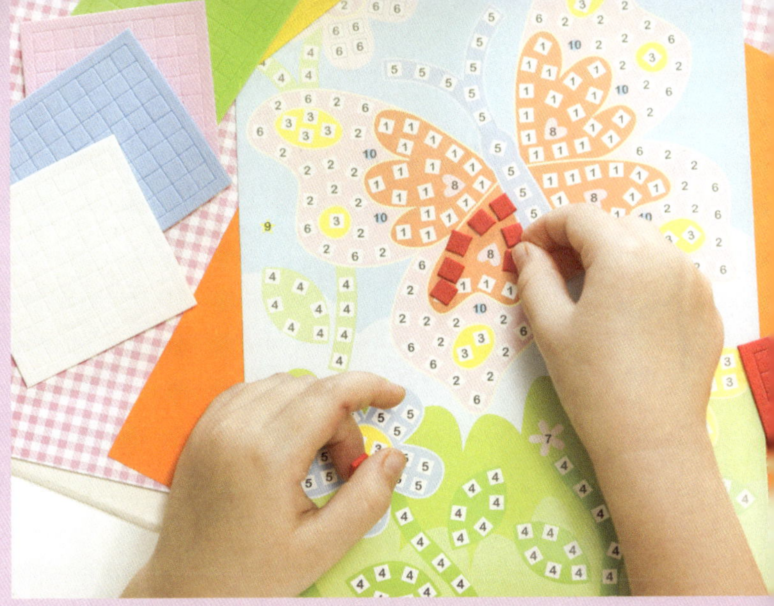

Mosaic sticker art is fun and easy. Just peel, stick, and enjoy!

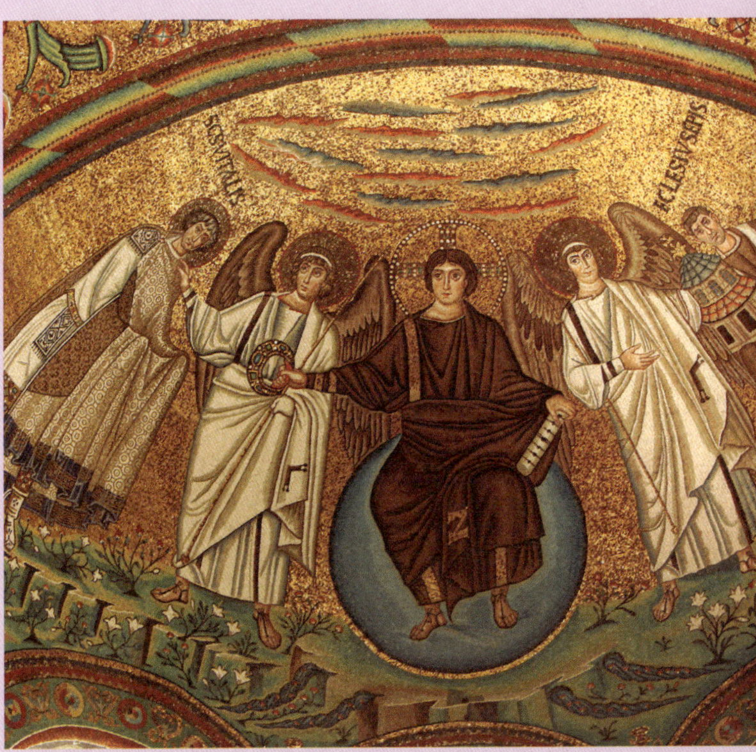

This is one of the San Vitale mosaics of Jesus Christ in Ravenna, Italy, made around 570 CE. Mosaics were created at an angle so that flickering candlelight could reflect in the glass, making the artwork glow.

Mosaic art is also very important to different cultures. Rio de Janeiro, Brazil, for example, is known for its vibrant street art, including mosaic art called *azulejos*. The colorful and bright mosaics cover buildings, streets, and plazas around the city, creating a strong sense of cultural identity! Mosaic art is important to Islamic culture as well—ancient and modern mosques and palaces are covered in tiled mosaic art featuring geometric designs and religious scenes.

Plenty of artists around the world create mosaic art of their favorite celebrities. A smaller part of mosaic art is mosaic portrait art—art of a specific person using a mixture of different materials. Since celebrities and pop culture have a large impact on our society, it makes sense that artists want to create art reflective of their favorite singer, actor, or cultural icon.

Pop Artist Jason Mecier creates one-of-a-kind outrageous mosaic portraits. He meticulously fabricates anybody out of anything, from Kevin Bacon out of bacon, to Dolly Parton made out of trash (right), and many other celebrities made out of their trash! Jason's artwork has been featured everywhere from *Entertainment Weekly* to *The New York Times*, on TV shows like *Glee*, *Rachael Ray*, and *TMZ*, as well as music videos by P!nk and Pitbull. His portraits are hanging in Ripley's Believe It or Not! museums and countless celebrity homes! Check out Jason's book, *Pop Trash*, available wherever books are sold.

So, whether you create mosaic art yourself with stickers and tiles, or you enjoy learning the history of this beautiful art form, mosaic art can teach you how to appreciate the small things—because when put together, little pieces create a stunning big picture!

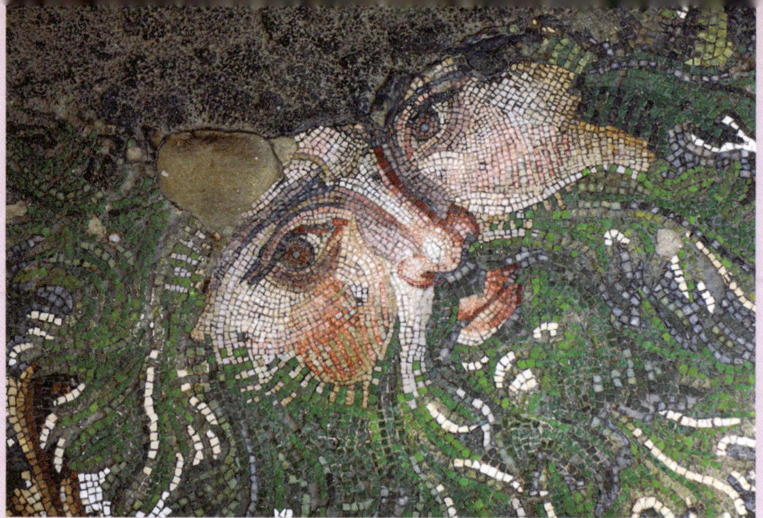

This ancient mosaic, a part of the Great Palace Mosaics Museum, dates back to the Byzantine period. It is in Istanbul, and was created in the sixth century CE.

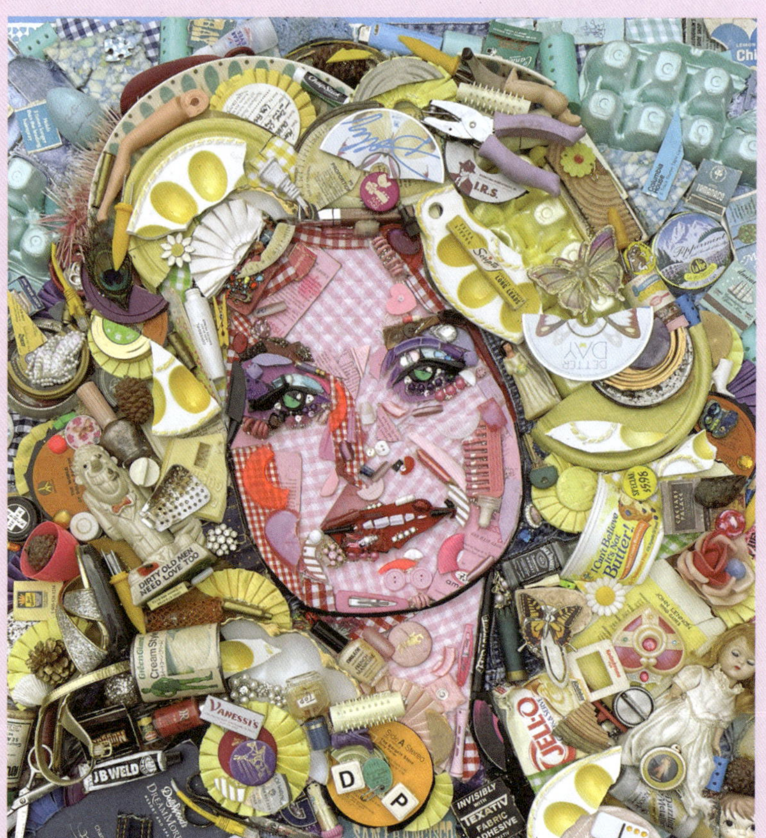

A mosaic art portrait made by Jason Mecier of Dolly Parton, entirely made of trash!

Dolly's Legacy

Dolly Parton is a name synonymous with talent, philanthropy, and timeless charm. From her humble beginnings in the Great Smoky Mountains to her status as a global icon, Dolly's journey is a testament to resilience, creativity, and the power of dreams. Her life story continues to inspire generations, and her recent resurgence in popularity has only solidified her place in the hearts of fans young and old.

Whether she's writing, performing, acting, giving, or smiling, Dolly has an effervescent glow that captures everyone around her. You may have heard of some of her famous sayings, like "Storms make trees take deeper roots," or "You'll never do a whole lot unless you're brave enough to try." Small inspirations like these come from Dolly's experience of overcoming hardship and her desire to help others who are experiencing the same slopes and valleys of life that she has.

Dolly's symbol, the butterfly, is a peaceful creature that is free to soar above the troubles of life. As you learn about Dolly—and create art inspired by her—keep the butterfly in mind, and let it bring some of Dolly's love into your life's journey. As Dolly says, "Love is like a butterfly, a rare and gentle thing."

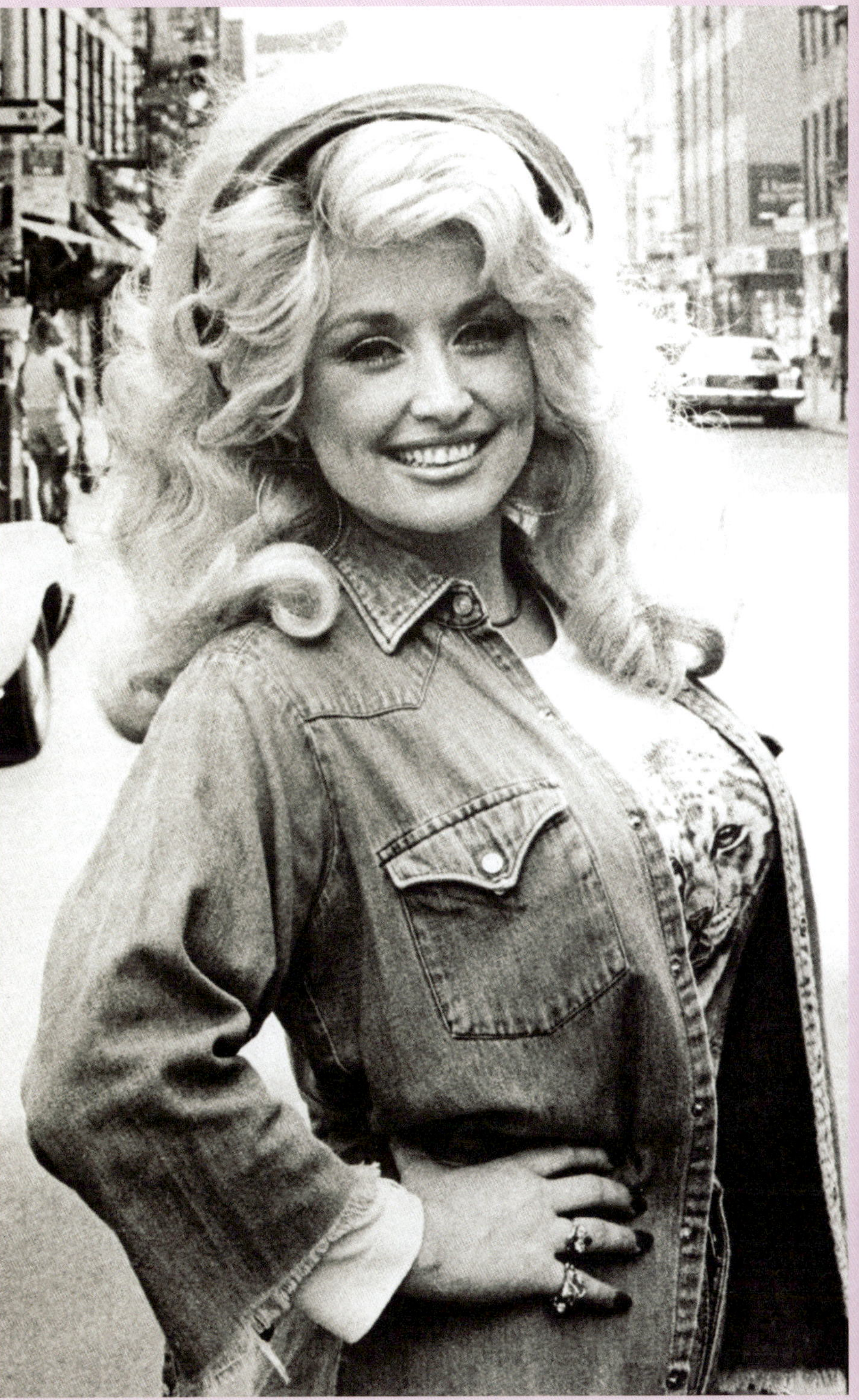

Dolly Parton is a national treasure and an inspiration that you can overcome anything if you never give up.

Early Life and Childhood (1946-1960)

Dolly Rebecca Parton was born on January 19, 1946, in a one-room cabin in Locust Ridge, Tennessee, a rural area nestled in the Great Smoky Mountains. As the fourth of twelve children, Dolly's early life was marked by the struggles and joys of growing up in a large, loving family. Her parents, Avie Lee Caroline Owens and Robert Lee Parton, were hardworking but financially challenged, and Dolly often recounts stories of her childhood with fondness despite the hardships.

Growing up in poverty, Dolly and her siblings often had to make do with very little. The family farm provided some food, but there were times when they had to rely on the kindness of neighbors and the community to get by. Dolly's father, Lee, worked multiple jobs to support the family, while her mother, Avie Lee, took care of the children and the household. Despite the financial struggles, Avie Lee's love for music and storytelling deeply influenced Dolly. She would often sing old folk songs and hymns to her children, planting the seeds of Dolly's musical future.

From a young age, Dolly showed an exceptional talent for music, influenced by her mother's folk songs and her grandfather's Pentecostal preaching. By the age of ten, she was performing on local radio and television shows, her vibrant personality and voice already captivating audiences. Her determination and passion for music set the stage for what would become a legendary career.

Dolly's siblings also played a significant role in her early musical experiences. The Parton children often sang together, and family gatherings were filled with music and laughter. These early experiences of performing with her family helped Dolly develop her stage presence and confidence. Dolly attended Sevier County High School, where she was known for her unique style and vibrant personality. Even then, she dreamed of making it big in the music industry. After graduating in 1964, she wasted no time and moved to Nashville, Tennessee, the heart of the country music industry.

Did You Know?

At just five years old, Dolly wrote her very first song titled "Little Tiny Tasseltop," inspired by her homemade corncob doll.

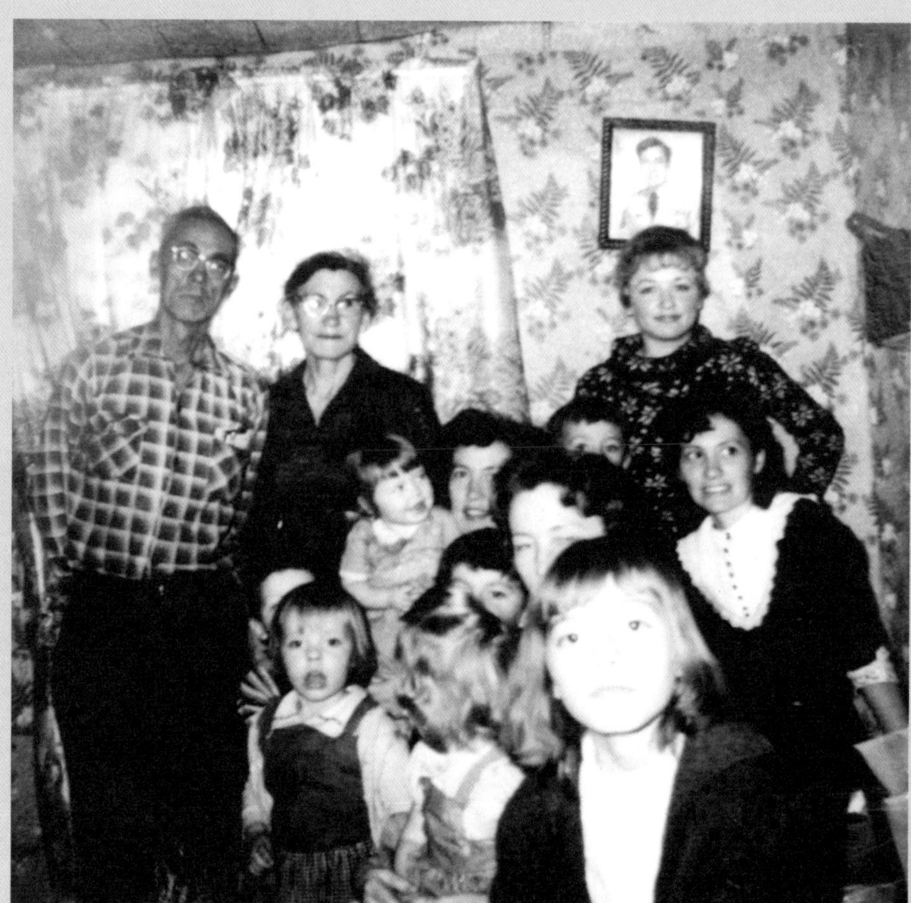

Dolly (upper right in back) with her family on Christmas, 1960.

Early Career and Breakthrough (1960-1970)

Dolly's initial years in Nashville were challenging, filled with small gigs and songwriting for other artists.

In 1967, she joined *The Porter Wagoner Show*, a pivotal moment that catapulted her into the national spotlight. As part of Porter Wagoner's show, Dolly gained widespread recognition, and their duet "The Last Thing on My Mind" became a significant hit.

Dolly and her future husband, Carl Dean, first met outside the Wishy Washy Laundromat in Nashville, Tennessee, on the day Dolly moved to the city in 1964. Carl, who was 21 at the time, caught sight of the 18-year-old Dolly and was instantly smitten. He approached her, saying, "You're gonna get sunburned out here, little lady." Dolly, charmed by his concern, replied, "Well, I'll burn later, but I'll talk to you now." The couple began dating and quickly fell in love. They were married on May 30, 1966, in a small, private ceremony in Ringgold, Georgia, with only Dolly's mother, Avie Lee Caroline, and the preacher and his wife in attendance.

Dolly's early years in Nashville were a mix of excitement and hardship. She signed with Monument Records in 1965, initially as a bubblegum pop singer. However, her heart was in country music, and she convinced the label to let her record country songs. Her first country single, "Dumb Blonde," released in 1967, became a Top 25 hit on the country charts, proving that she was more than just a pretty face. Her unique voice, combined with her knack for storytelling, set her apart in the competitive country music scene. By the end of the decade, Dolly Parton had firmly established herself as a rising star. Dolly's early career was marked by her prolific songwriting. She penned many songs for other artists, honing her craft and developing her distinctive style. Her songwriting ability caught the attention of industry insiders, and she quickly became known for her lyrical prowess and ability to tell compelling stories through music.

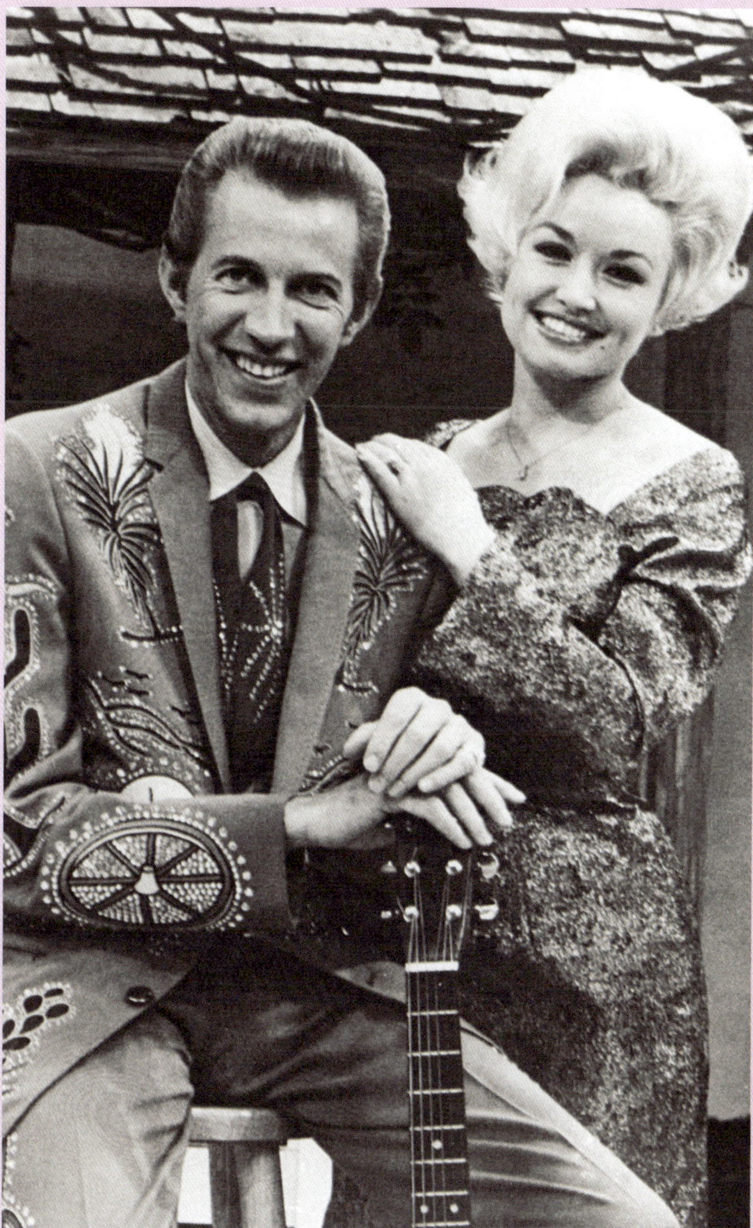

Dolly and Porter Wagoner on *The Porter Wagoner Show*, 1972.

Establishing Stardom (1970-1980)

The 1970s marked Dolly Parton's transition from a country singer to a mainstream superstar. Her decision to pursue a solo career proved fruitful, with hits like "Jolene" (1973) and "I Will Always Love You" (1974) becoming iconic songs that transcended genres. These tracks showcased her emotional depth and vocal prowess, earning her critical acclaim and a growing fan base.

Dolly's success wasn't confined to music alone. She ventured into television, starring in her own variety show *Dolly* and making guest appearances on various programs. Her charisma and wit endeared her to audiences, and she seamlessly blended her musical and acting talents. In 1978, Dolly's crossover appeal was solidified when she won her first Grammy Award for Best Female Country Vocal Performance for "Here You Come Again." Her ability to navigate different genres and mediums was a testament to her versatility and drive.

During this decade, Dolly also made the bold decision to leave *The Porter Wagoner Show* and focus on her solo career. The transition was not without its challenges, as she had to prove herself as an independent artist. "Jolene," released in 1973, was a turning point, showcasing her songwriting prowess and unique voice. The song's haunting melody and compelling lyrics made it an instant classic.

"I Will Always Love You," written as a farewell to Porter Wagoner, further cemented her status as a solo artist. The song's heartfelt lyrics and Dolly's soulful delivery resonated with listeners, and it became one of her most enduring hits. Whitney Houston's 1992 cover of the song brought it international fame, but Dolly's original remains a beloved classic.

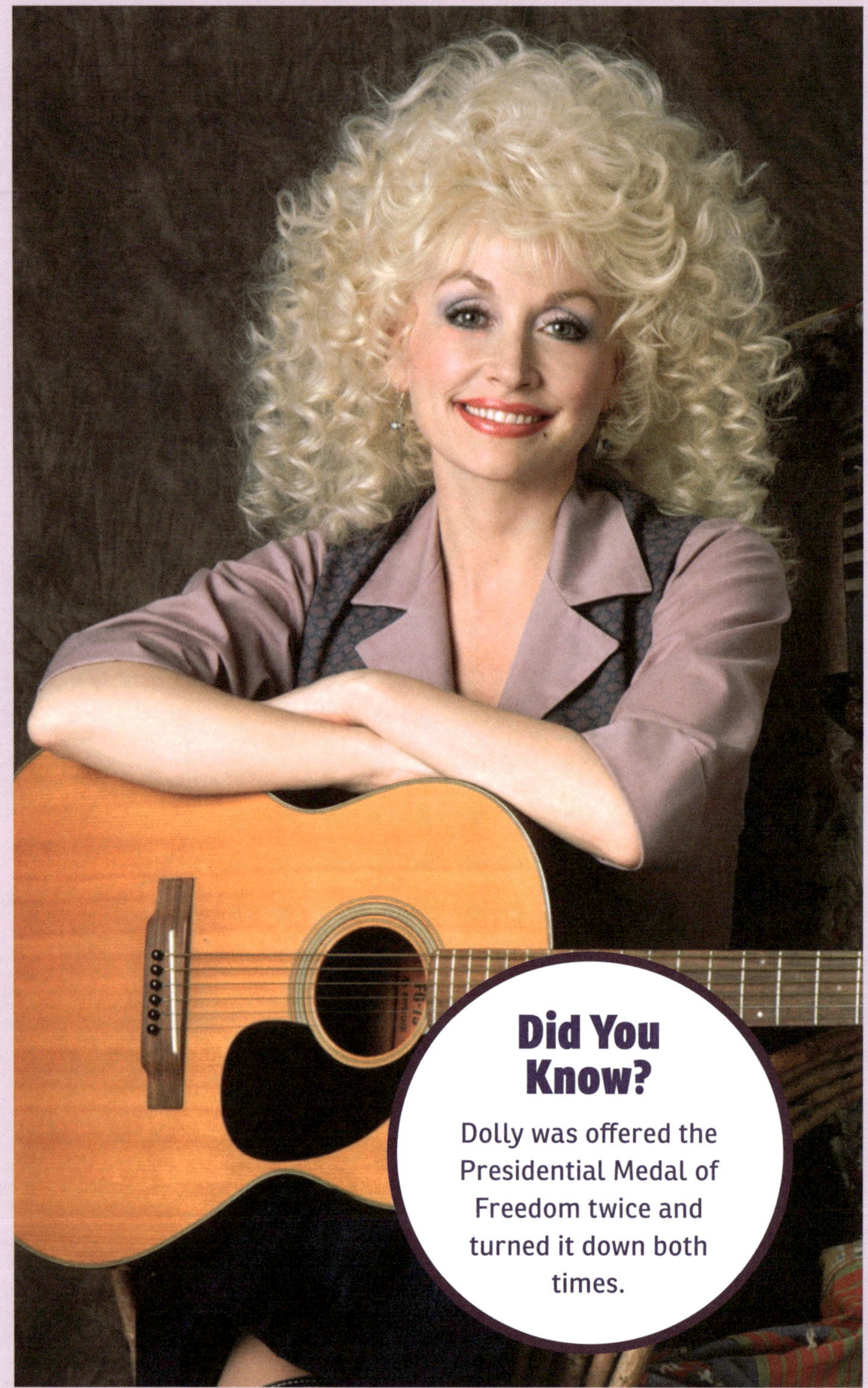

Did You Know?

Dolly was offered the Presidential Medal of Freedom twice and turned it down both times.

Dolly for her variety show, *Dolly*.

Broadening Horizons (1980-1990)

The 1980s saw Dolly Parton expanding her horizons even further. Her starring role in the 1980 film *9 to 5*, alongside Jane Fonda and Lily Tomlin, was a major success, earning her critical praise and a Golden Globe nomination. The film's title song, written and performed by Dolly, became an anthem for working women and earned her two Grammy awards. Dolly became a fashion icon, known for her glamorous style and signature big hair. Her unique look and bold fashion choices made her a trendsetter, and she inspired countless fans to embrace their individuality and express themselves through fashion.

Dolly continued to release hit albums, with songs like "Islands in the Stream" (a duet with Kenny Rogers) topping the charts. Her appeal extended beyond country music, and she became a beloved figure in pop culture.

In 1986, Dolly opened Dollywood®, a theme park in Pigeon Forge, Tennessee, celebrating the culture and heritage of the Smoky Mountains. The park became a major tourist attraction and a source of pride for Dolly, reflecting her love for her roots and her desire to give back to her community. Dollywood was a culmination of Dolly's dream to create a place that celebrated the culture of the Smoky Mountains. The park features rides, attractions, and shows that highlight the region's music and crafts. Dollywood has grown over the years, attracting millions of visitors and becoming one of the most popular tourist destinations in the Southeast United States.

She established the Dollywood Foundation in 1988, focusing on education and literacy. One of the foundation's most notable programs, the Imagination Library, would be launched in 1995. To date, the Imagination Library has distributed millions of books worldwide. She also launched a successful line of cake and baking mixes, dog clothes and accessories, and other merchandise, expanding her brand and reaching new audiences.

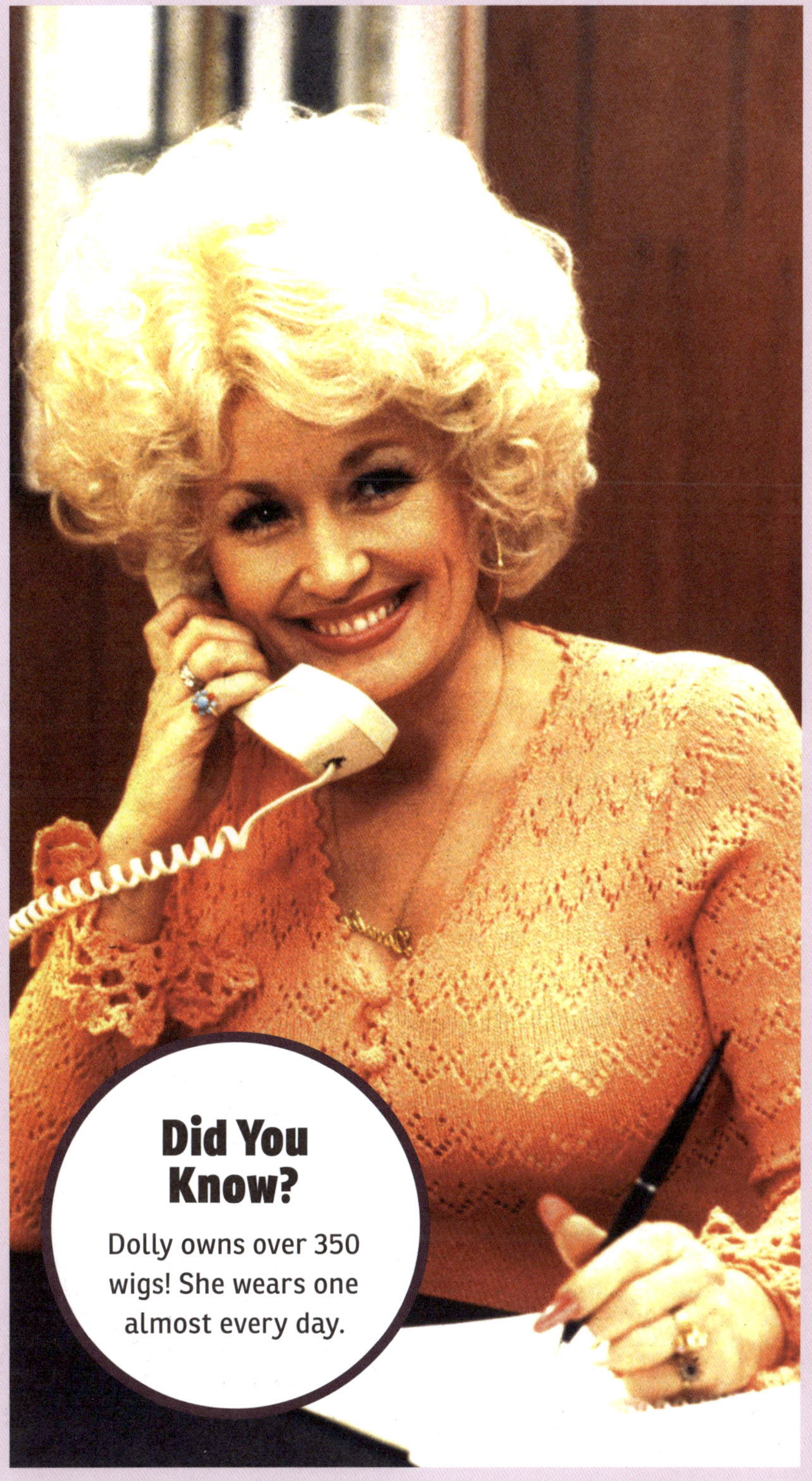

Did You Know?

Dolly owns over 350 wigs! She wears one almost every day.

Dolly on set of the movie *9 to 5*, where she played Doralee Rhodes.

Continued Success and Reinvention (late 1980s-2000)

Dolly Parton's career showed no signs of slowing down. She continued to release successful albums and collaborate with a diverse array of artists. Her music evolved with the times, but her authentic voice and storytelling remained consistent. In addition to her musical achievements, Dolly's acting career flourished. She starred in films like *Steel Magnolias* (1989) and *Straight Talk* (1992), showcasing her versatility as an actress. Her performances were praised for their warmth and humor, further cementing her status as a multifaceted entertainer.

The 1990s also saw Dolly exploring new musical territories. She released several bluegrass albums, including *The Grass is Blue* (1999), which received critical acclaim and won a Grammy Award. This success was followed by more bluegrass projects, including *Little Sparrow* (2001) and *Halos & Horns* (2002), both of which were well-received by critics and fans alike. Dolly proved that she could reinvent herself and stay relevant in a rapidly changing music industry. Her collaborations with other artists also highlighted her versatility. She worked with Vince Gill, Ricky Skaggs, and Emmylou Harris, among others, producing music that resonated with fans across genres. Her ability to bridge the gap between traditional country, bluegrass, and contemporary music showcased her enduring talent and adaptability.

Dolly's acting career also continued to thrive during the 1990s. Her role in *Steel Magnolias* was particularly notable, earning her praise for her portrayal of Truvy Jones, a kind-hearted and sassy beauty salon owner. The film's success further cemented Dolly's status as a versatile entertainer capable of delivering compelling performances in both comedic and dramatic roles.

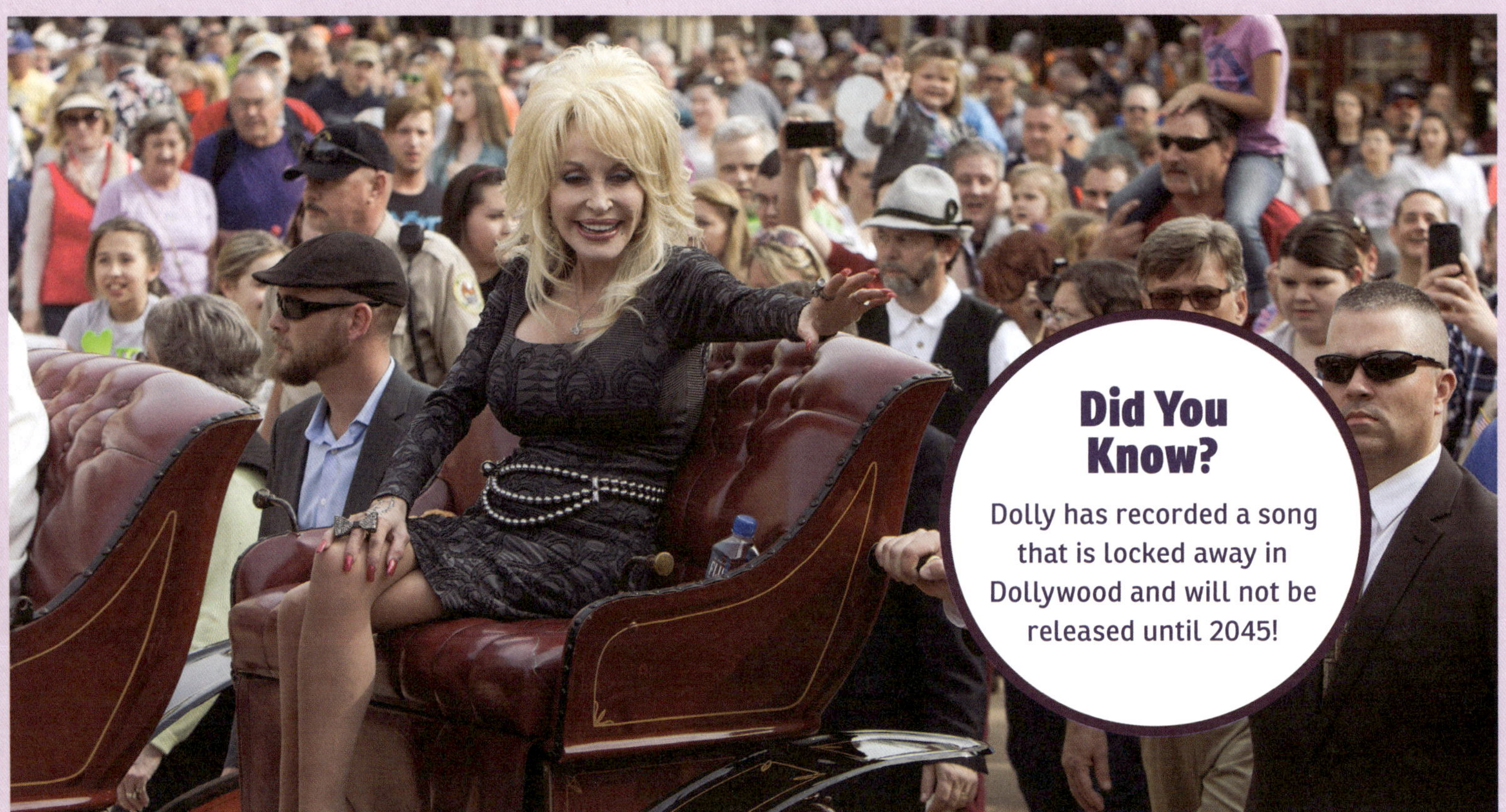

Dolly at a parade in Dollywood, waving to fans.

Did You Know?

Dolly has recorded a song that is locked away in Dollywood and will not be released until 2045!

Modern Era and Resurgence (2000-Present)

The new millennium brought a resurgence in Dolly Parton's popularity. Her work earned numerous awards and accolades, including induction into the Country Music Hall of Fame in 1999. Dolly's appeal extended to a younger generation, thanks in part to her involvement in contemporary projects. In 2018, she contributed to the soundtrack of the Netflix film *Dumplin'*, which featured a collection of her classic hits and new material. The song "Girl in the Movies" received a Golden Globe nomination, showcasing Dolly's continued relevance and appeal.

In 2020, Dolly released the holiday album *A Holly Dolly Christmas*, which topped the *Billboard* Country Albums chart, demonstrating her enduring popularity. She also starred in the Netflix holiday special *Christmas on the Square*, which won a Primetime Emmy Award for Outstanding Television Movie.

In addition to her music and philanthropy, Dolly has remained active in the entertainment industry. She produced and starred in the Netflix anthology series *Dolly Parton's Heartstrings*, which premiered in 2019. The series, inspired by her songs, received positive reviews for its heartfelt storytelling and showcased Dolly's multifaceted talents.

Her resilience, creativity, and kindness have made her a role model for women and men alike. In 2021, Dolly was honored with the Carnegie Medal of Philanthropy, recognizing her extensive charitable work and dedication to improving the lives of others. Dolly's recent endeavors also include her participation in social and political causes. She has been an advocate for LGBTQ+ rights, promoting acceptance and equality. Her inclusive stance and support for marginalized communities have further endeared her to fans of all ages.

In 2022, Dolly was inducted into the Rock & Roll Hall of Fame, a testament to her wide-ranging influence and contributions to the music industry. This recognition solidified her status as a versatile artist who has transcended genre boundaries and left an indelible mark on the world of music. Dolly Parton's life story is an inspiration to fans worldwide, showcasing the power of resilience, kindness, and staying true to oneself in the face of adversity. Her music, philanthropy, and unwavering spirit continue to touch hearts and inspire generations to dream big and never give up.

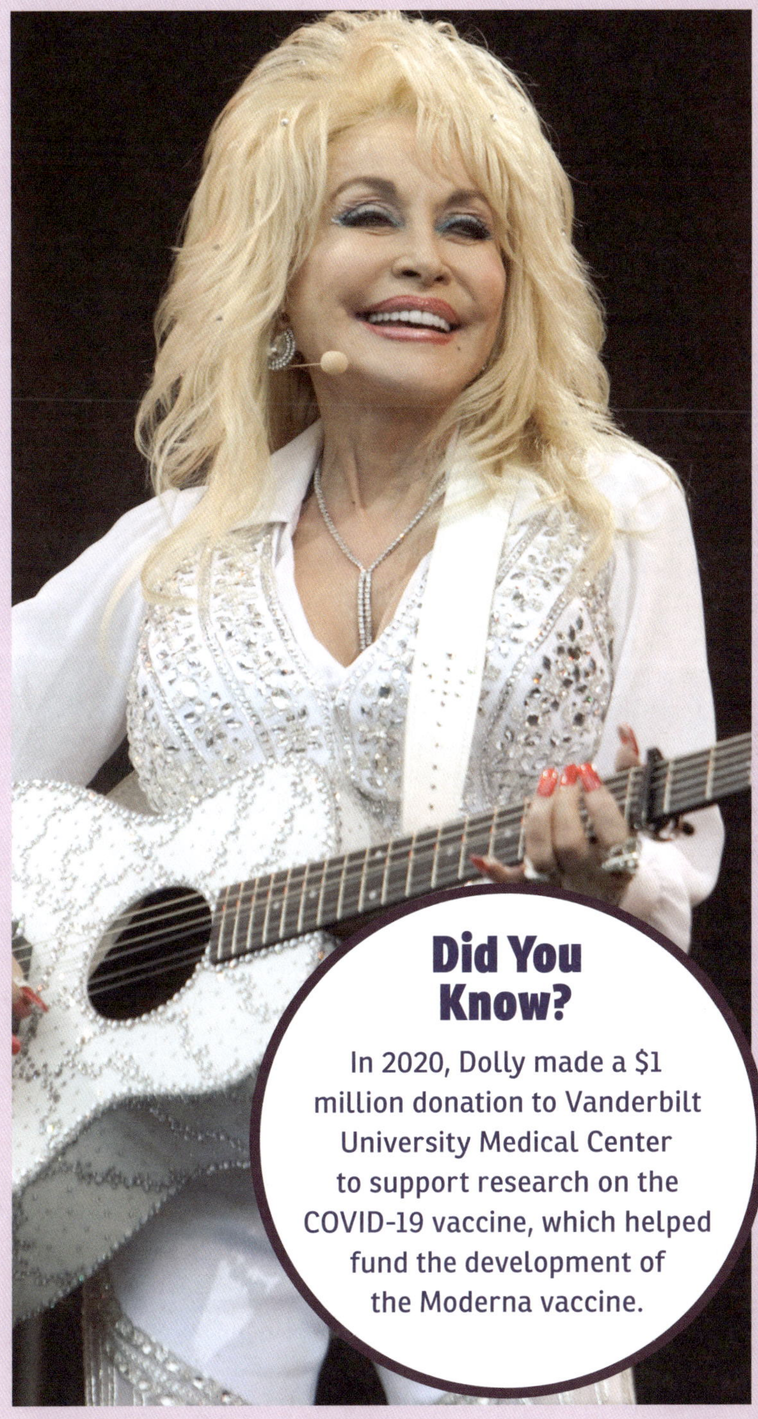

Did You Know?

In 2020, Dolly made a $1 million donation to Vanderbilt University Medical Center to support research on the COVID-19 vaccine, which helped fund the development of the Moderna vaccine.

Dolly singing the iconic song "Jolene" to an adoring crowd in 2014.

Great Movie Moments

9 to 5 (1980)

In her film debut, Dolly stars alongside Jane Fonda and Lily Tomlin in this classic comedy about three working women who turn the tables on their tyrannical boss. The film was a major success and remains a beloved classic.

Steel Magnolias (1989)

In this ensemble cast film, Dolly plays Truvy Jones, a kind-hearted beauty salon owner. The film, also starring Sally Field, Julia Roberts, and Shirley MacLaine, is a heartwarming and emotional story about the lives of women in a small Southern town.

Rhinestone (1984)

Dolly stars opposite Sylvester Stallone in this comedy about a country singer who bets that she can turn a New York City cabbie into a country music star. The film is known for its humor and Dolly's musical contributions.

Straight Talk (1992)

Dolly plays a small-town woman who accidentally becomes a popular radio talk show host in Chicago. Her performance as Shirlee Kenyon is both charming and entertaining.

Joyful Noise (2012)

Dolly stars alongside Queen Latifah in this musical comedy-drama about a small-town church choir competing in a national competition. The film features several musical performances by Dolly.

Unlikely Angel (1996)

In this made-for-TV Christmas movie, Dolly plays a country singer who, after dying in a car accident, is sent back to Earth as an angel to help a family in need. It's a heartwarming holiday film with Dolly's signature touch.

A Smoky Mountain Christmas (1986)

Another made-for-TV movie, this Christmas film features Dolly as a country singer who escapes to a mountain cabin for the holidays and ends up helping a group of orphans. It's a charming and festive movie.

Wild Texas Wind (1991)

Dolly stars as a country singer whose life takes a dramatic turn when she becomes involved in a violent relationship. The film is known for its strong performances and gripping storyline.

Dolly Parton's Coat of Many Colors (2015)

This made-for-TV movie is based on Dolly's autobiographical song and tells the story of her childhood in rural Tennessee. It was well-received for its heartfelt portrayal of Dolly's early life and family.

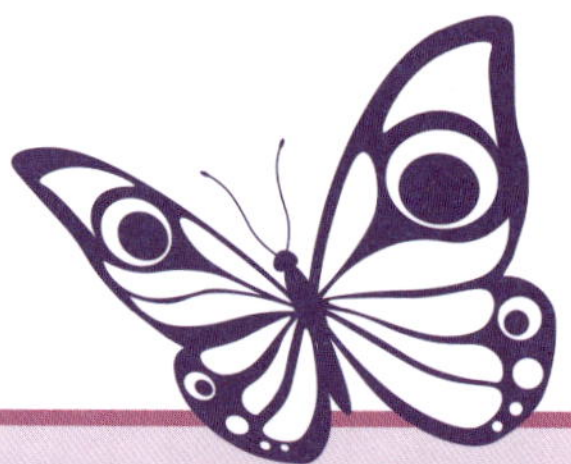

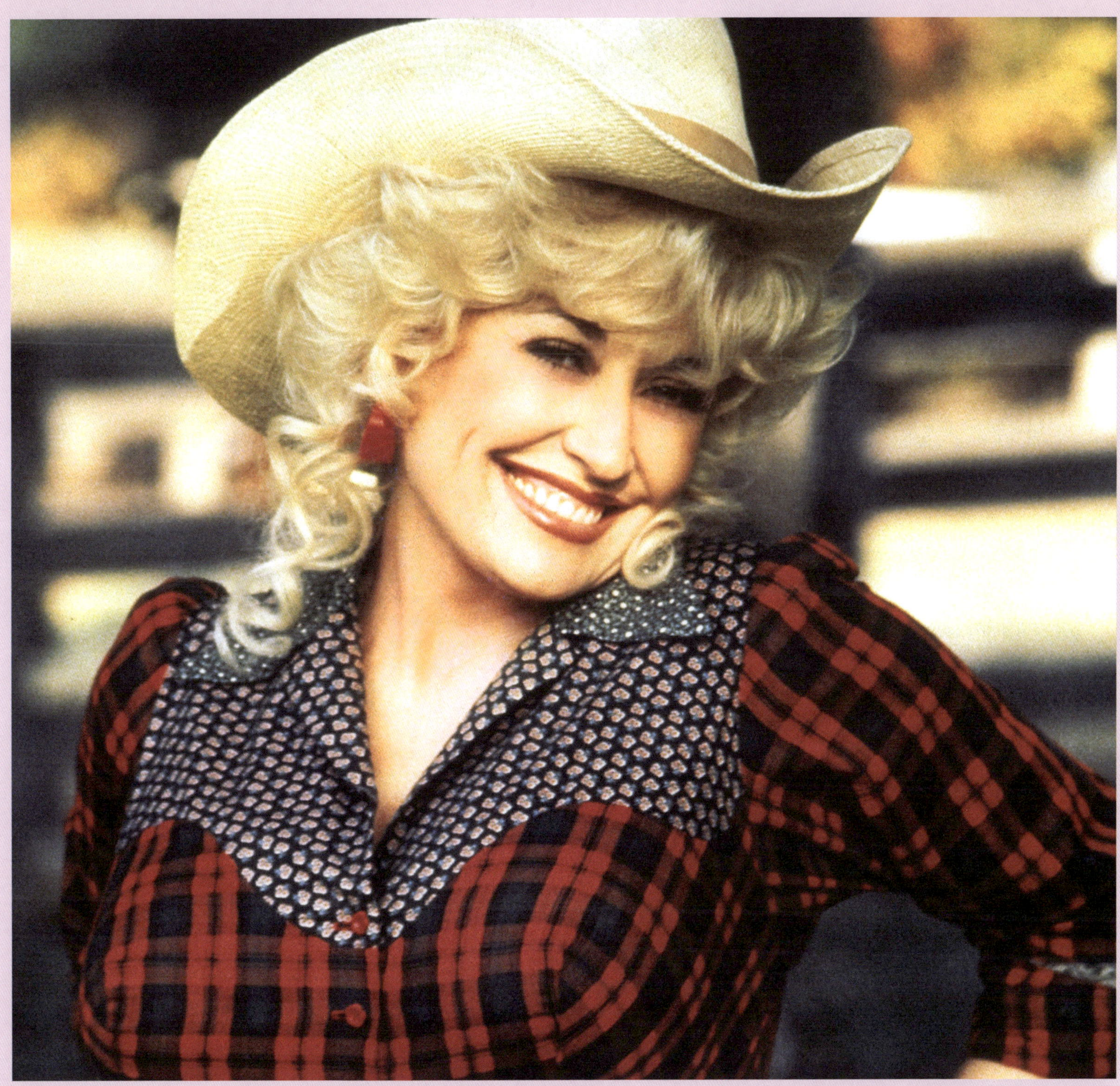

Dolly Parton in the movie *Rhinestone*, 1984. **Sticker this moment on page 23**.

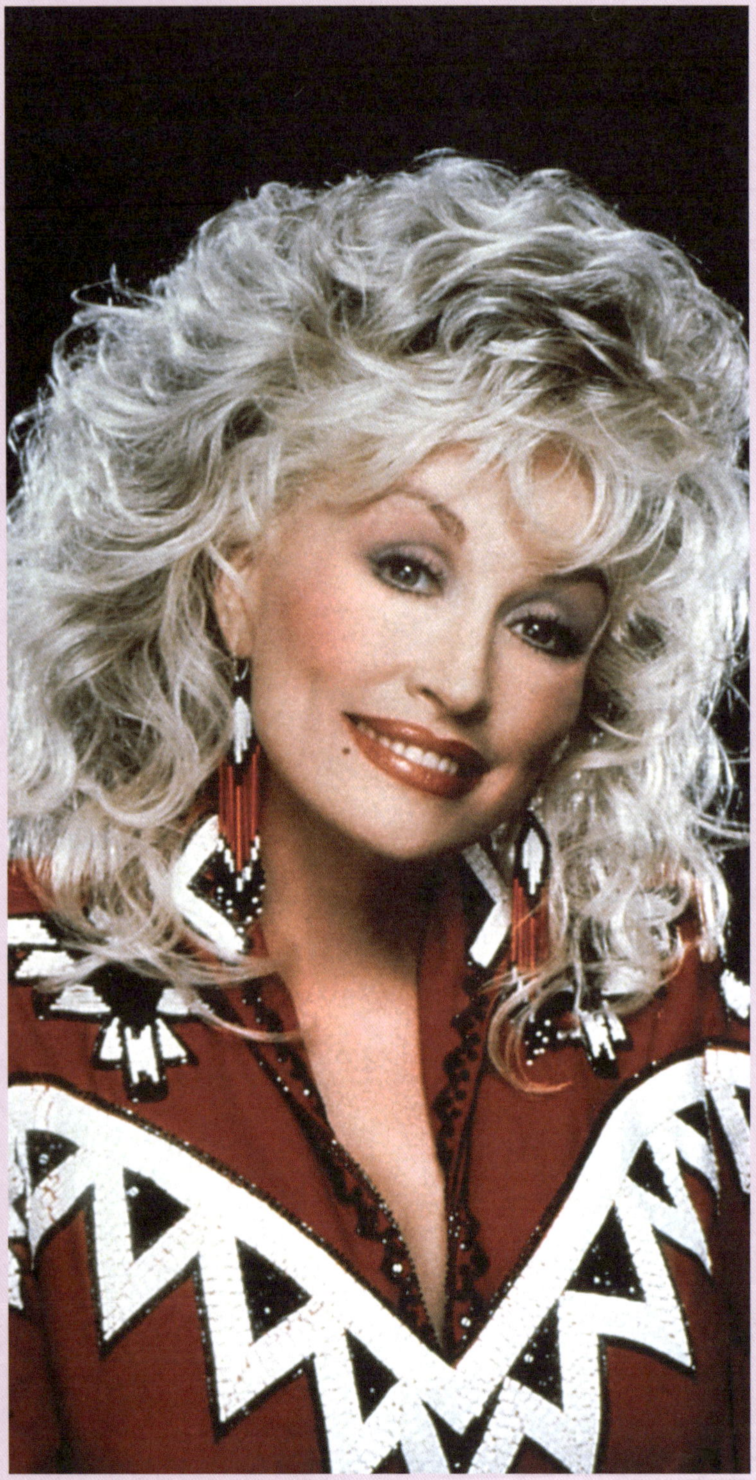

Dolly looking stunning in a country-western ensemble. **Sticker this moment on page 25**.

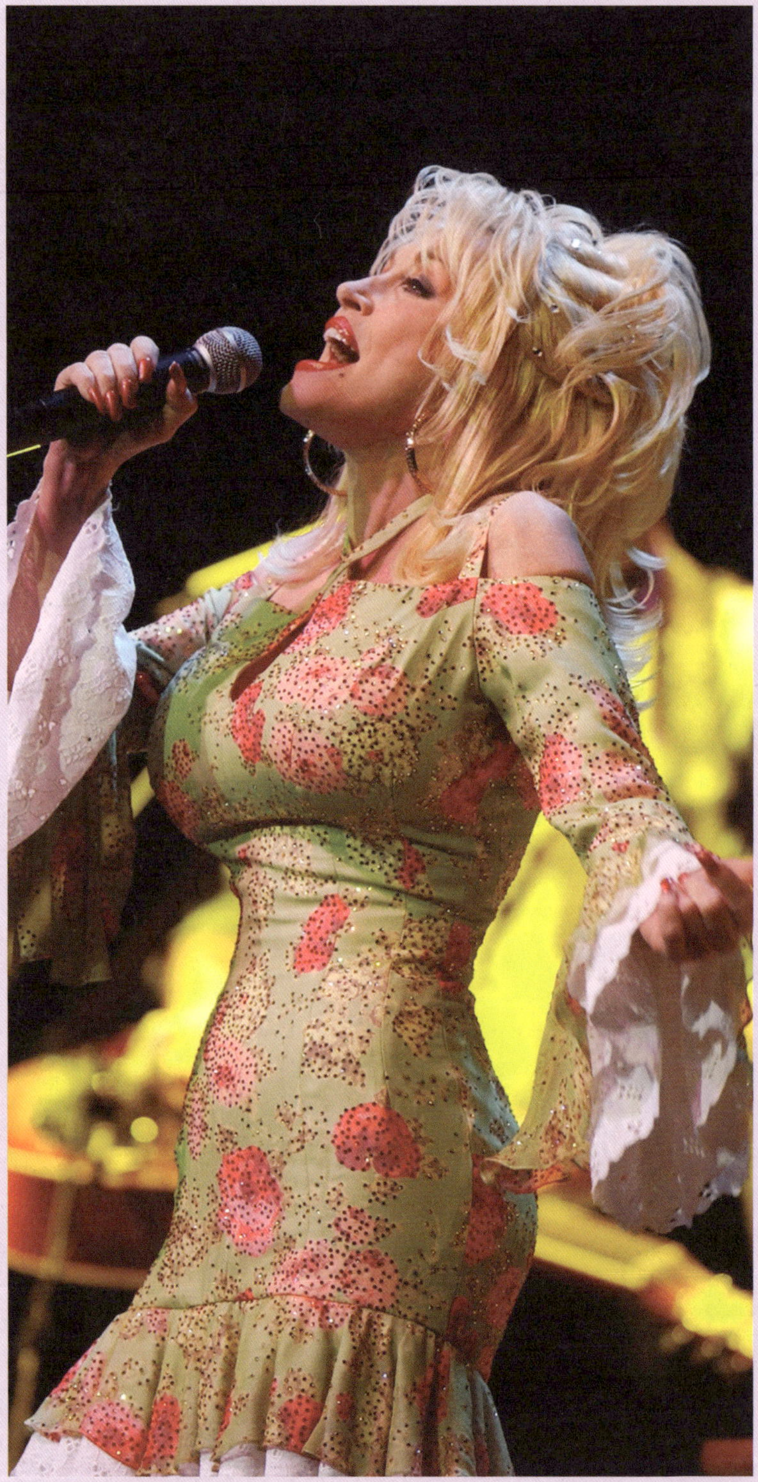

Dolly performing at the Clyde Auditorium in Glasgow, 2002. **Sticker this moment on page 27**.

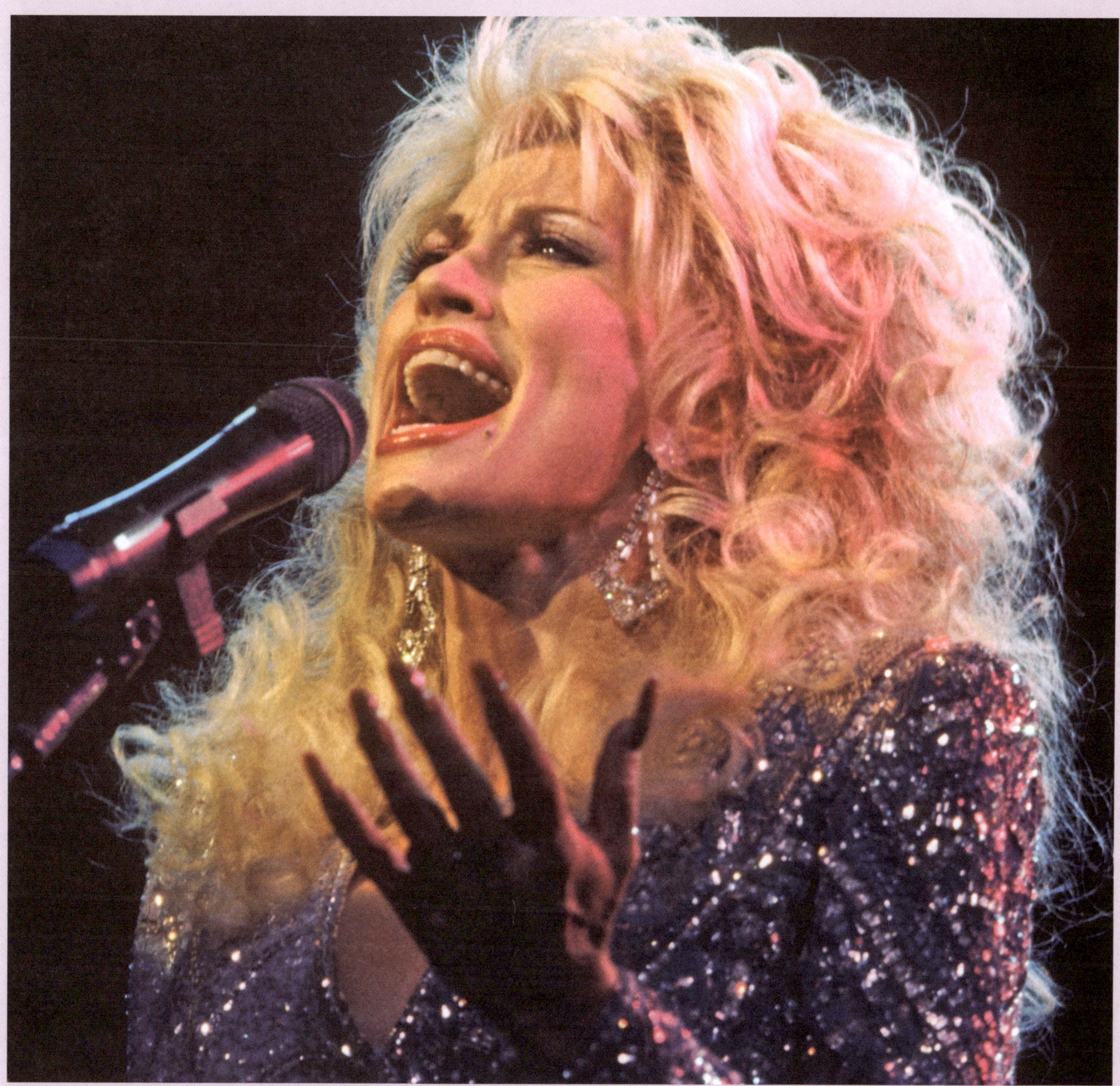

Dolly performing in 1989. **Sticker this moment on page 31**.

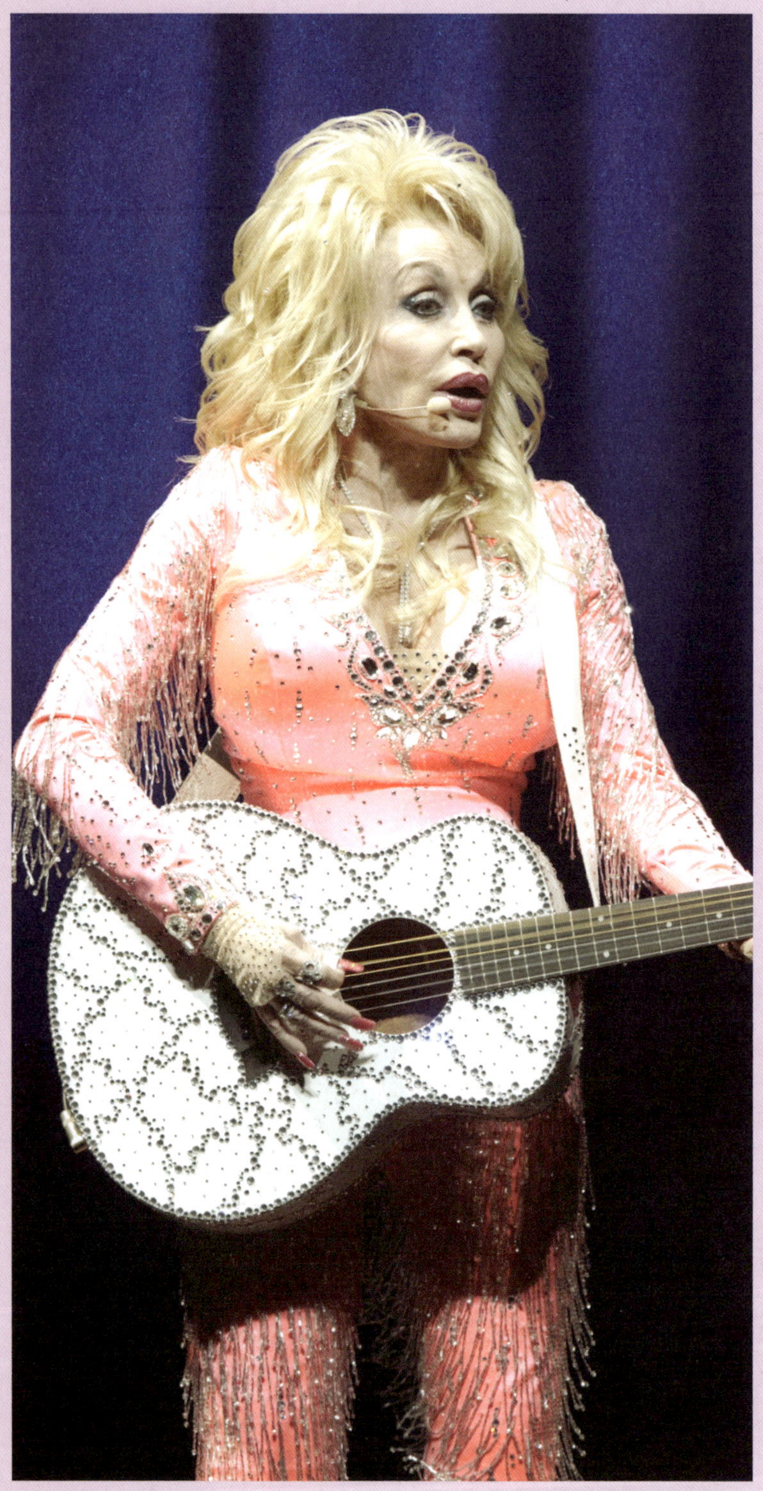

Dolly performing in Pittsburgh, Pennsylvania in 2016. **Sticker this moment on page 29**.

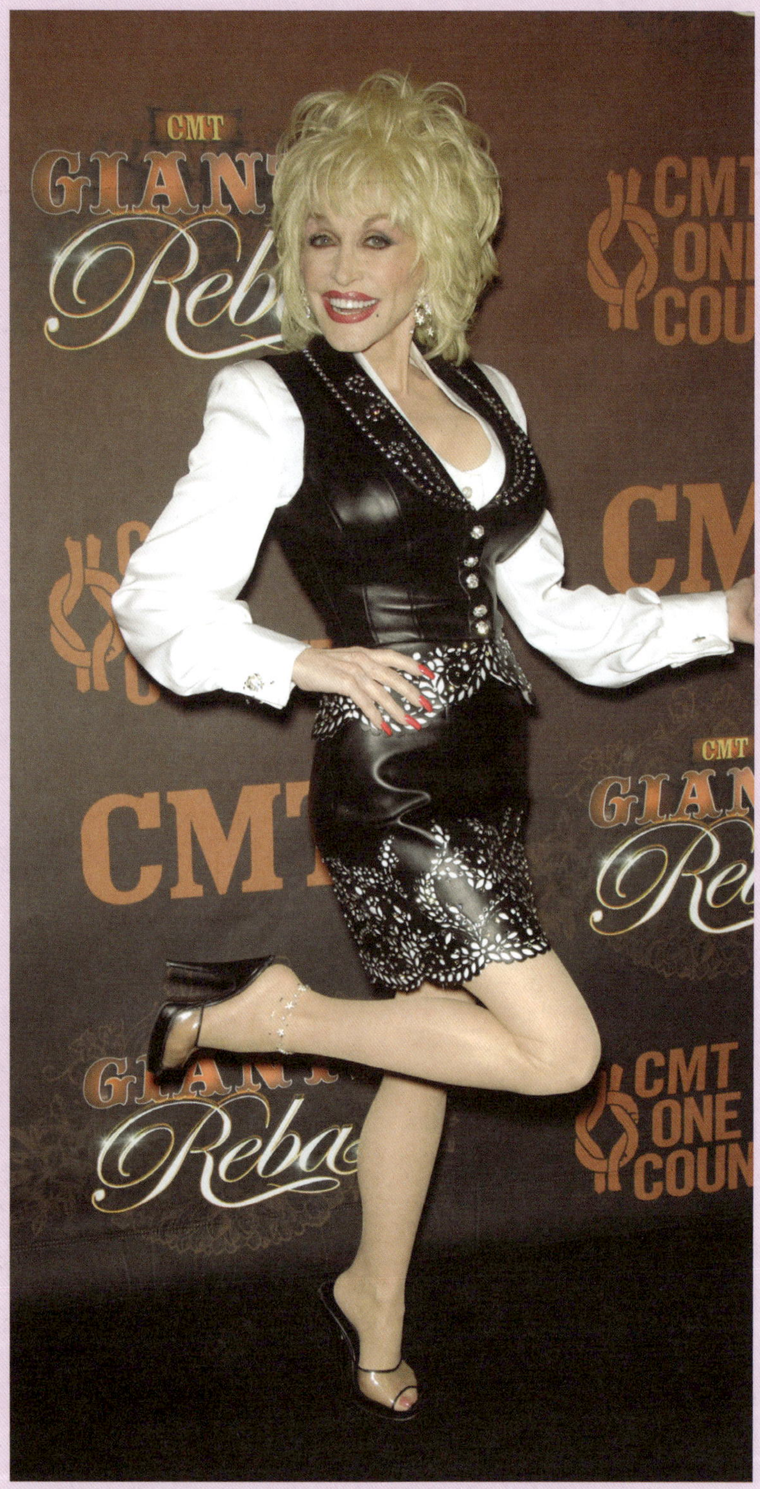

Dolly at the CMT Giants concert honoring Reba McEntire in 2006. **Sticker this moment on page 33**.

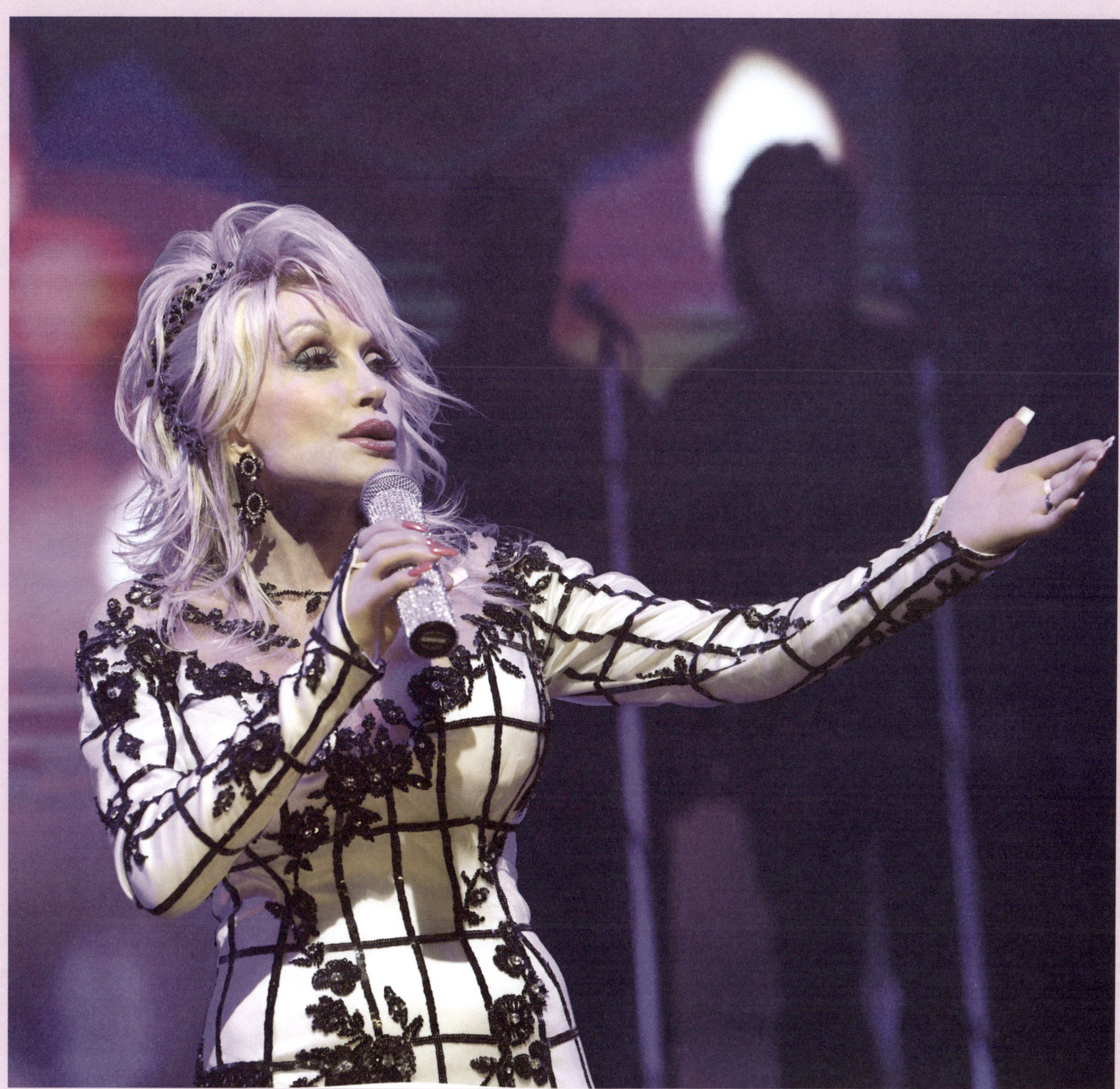

Dolly singing in *Dolly Parton's Mountain Magic Christmas*. **Sticker this moment on page 39**.

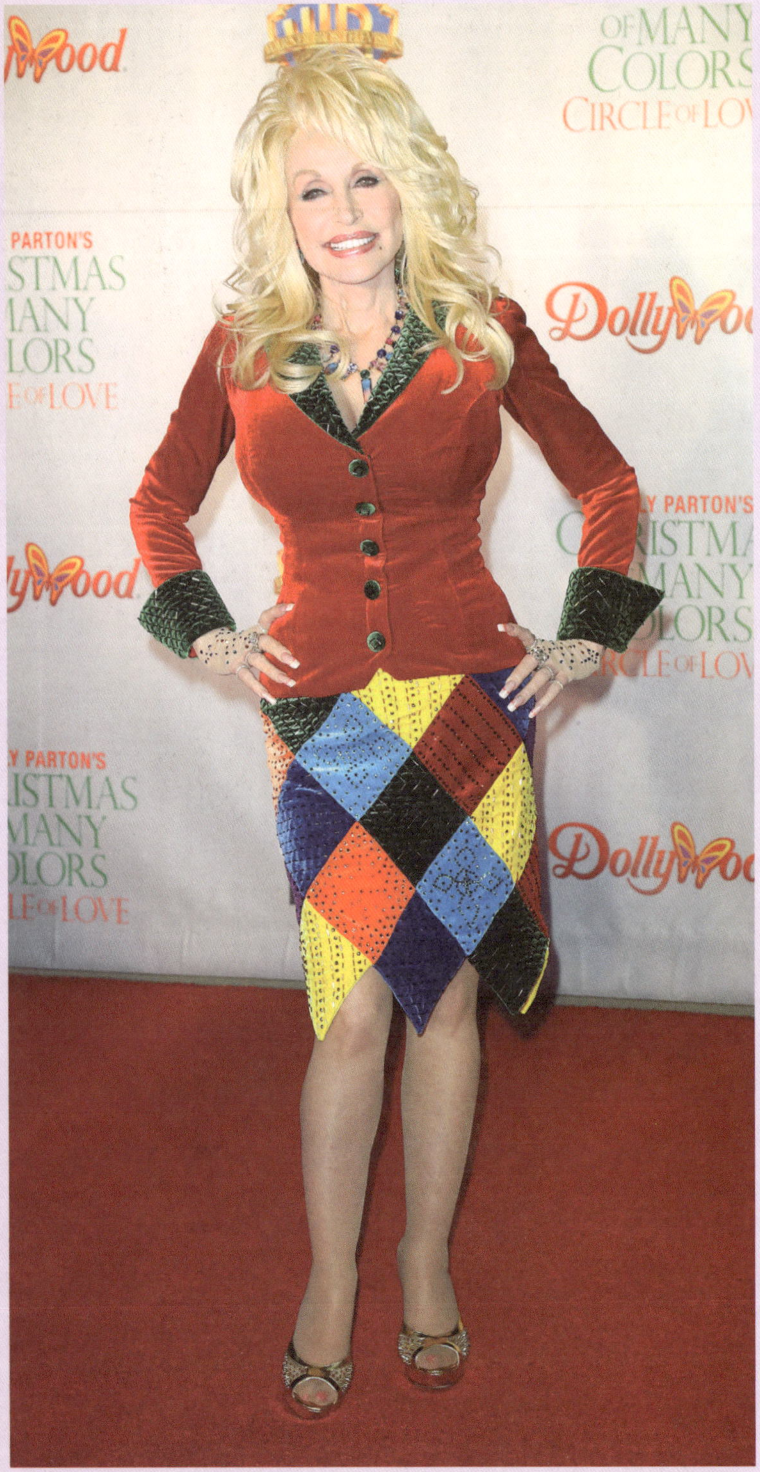

Dolly on the red carpet for *Dolly Parton's Christmas of Many Colors: Circle of Love*. **Sticker this moment on page 37**.

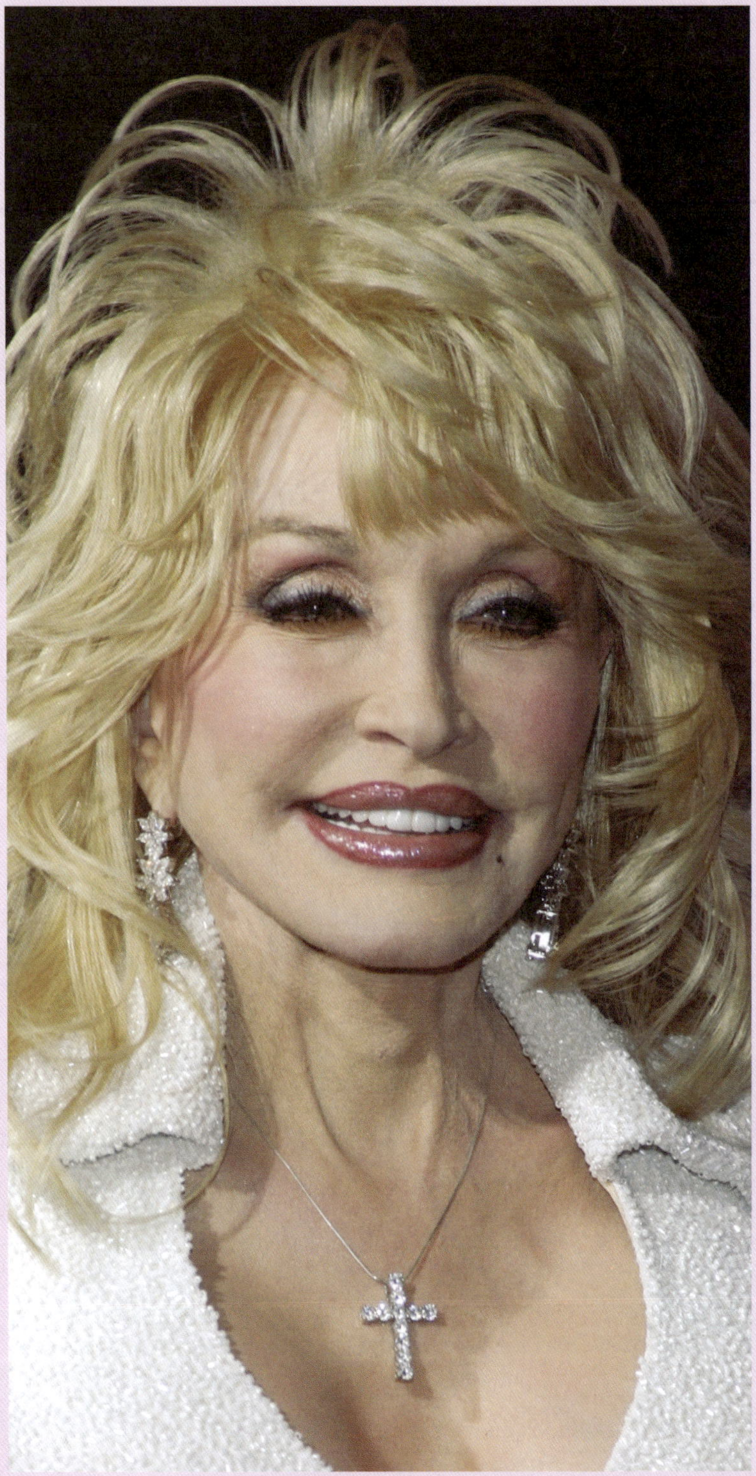

Dolly at the premiere of *Joyful Noise*, 2012. **Sticker this moment on page 35**.

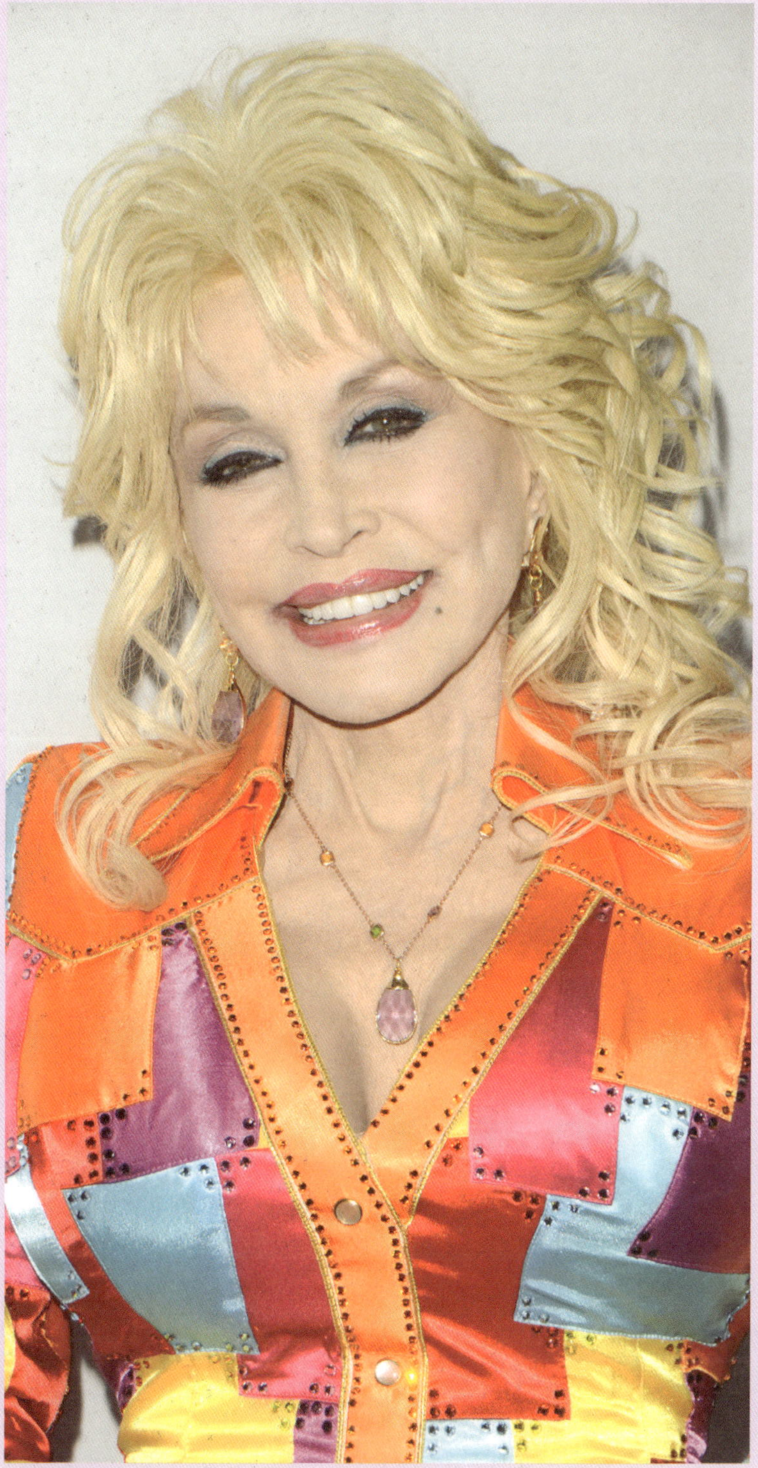

Dolly promoting *Dolly Parton's Coat of Many Colors*. **Sticker this moment on page 41**.

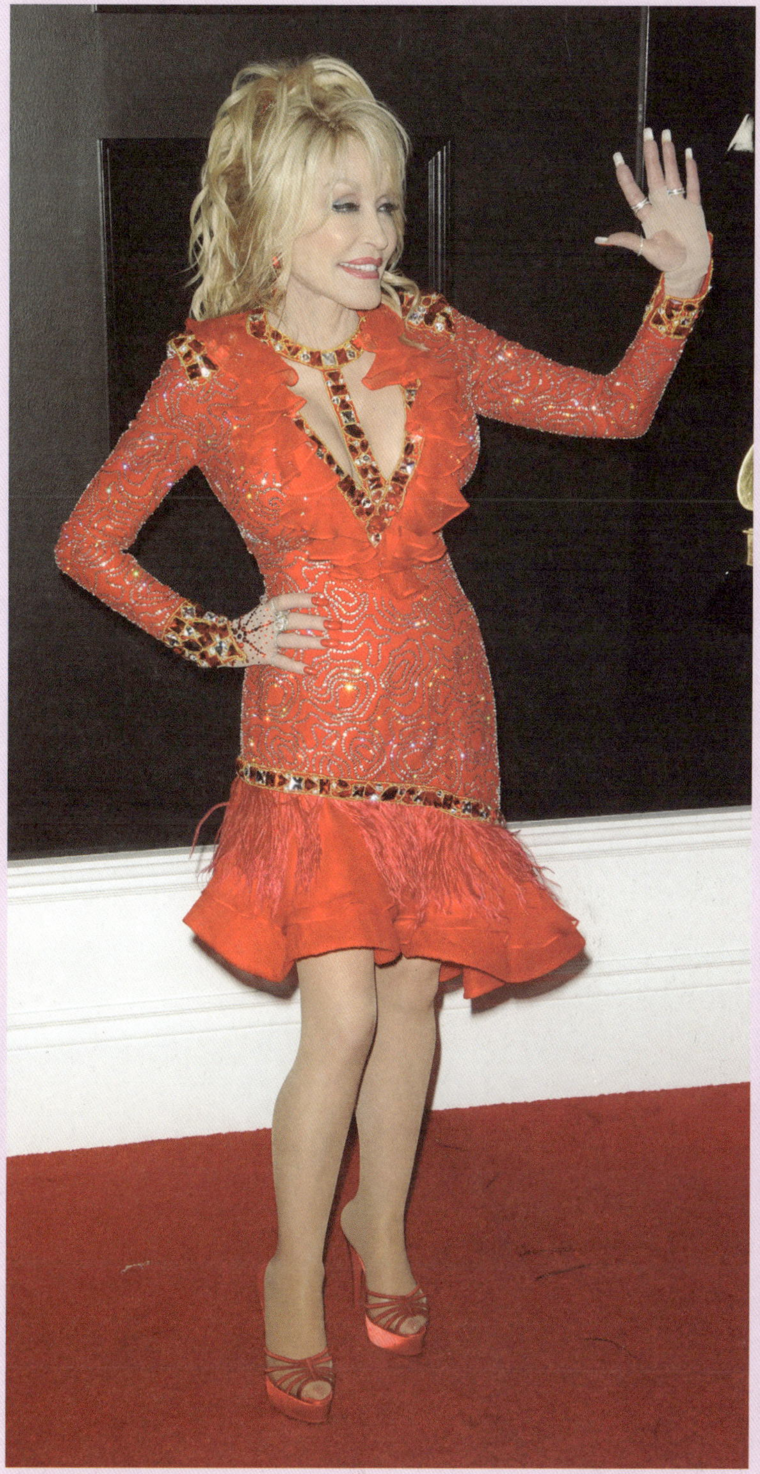

Dolly on the red carpet at the 2019 Grammy Awards. **Sticker this moment on page 45**.

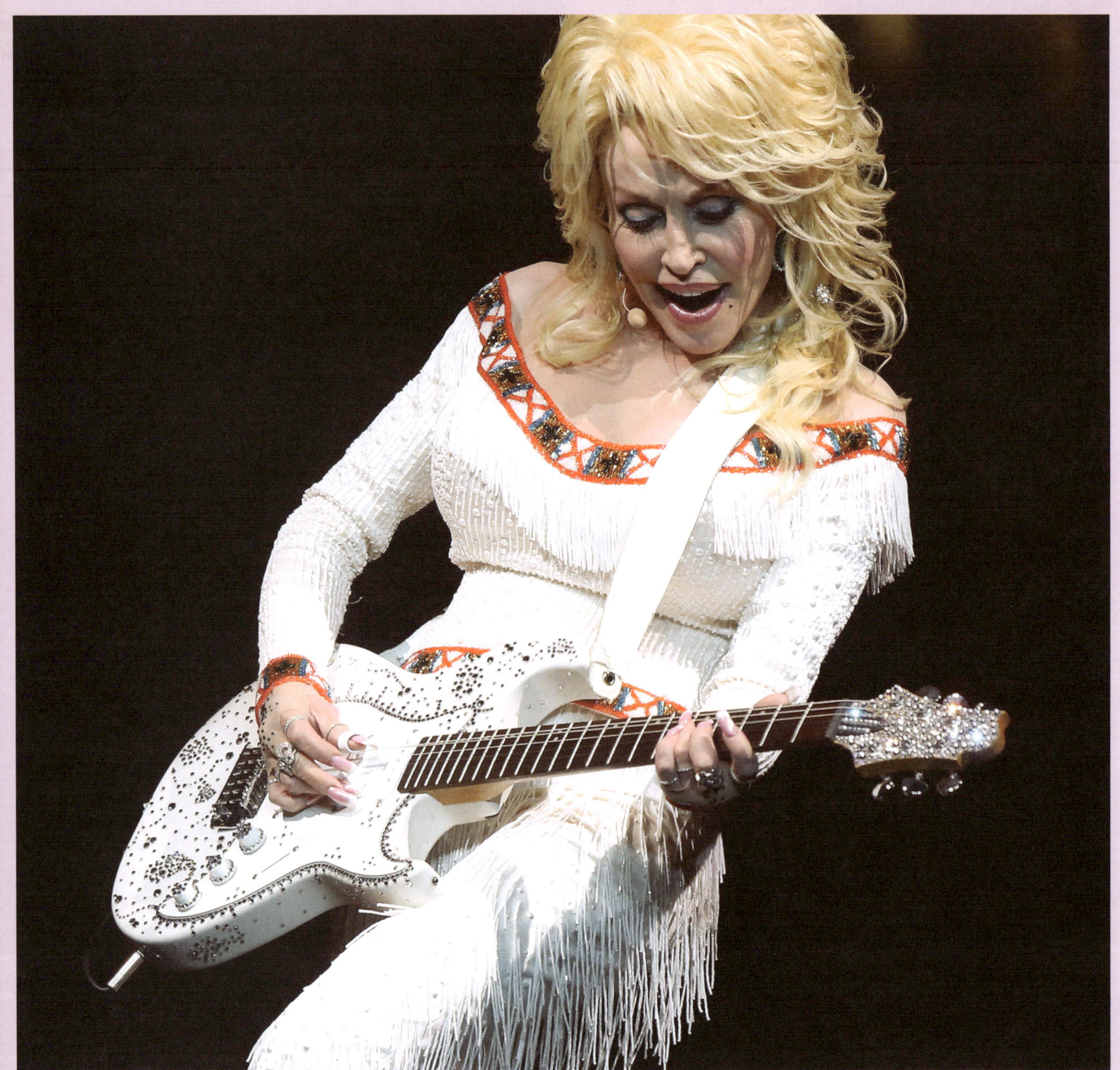

Dolly performing at her *Pure and Simple Tour* in 2016. **Sticker this moment on page 43**.

DOLLY PARTON

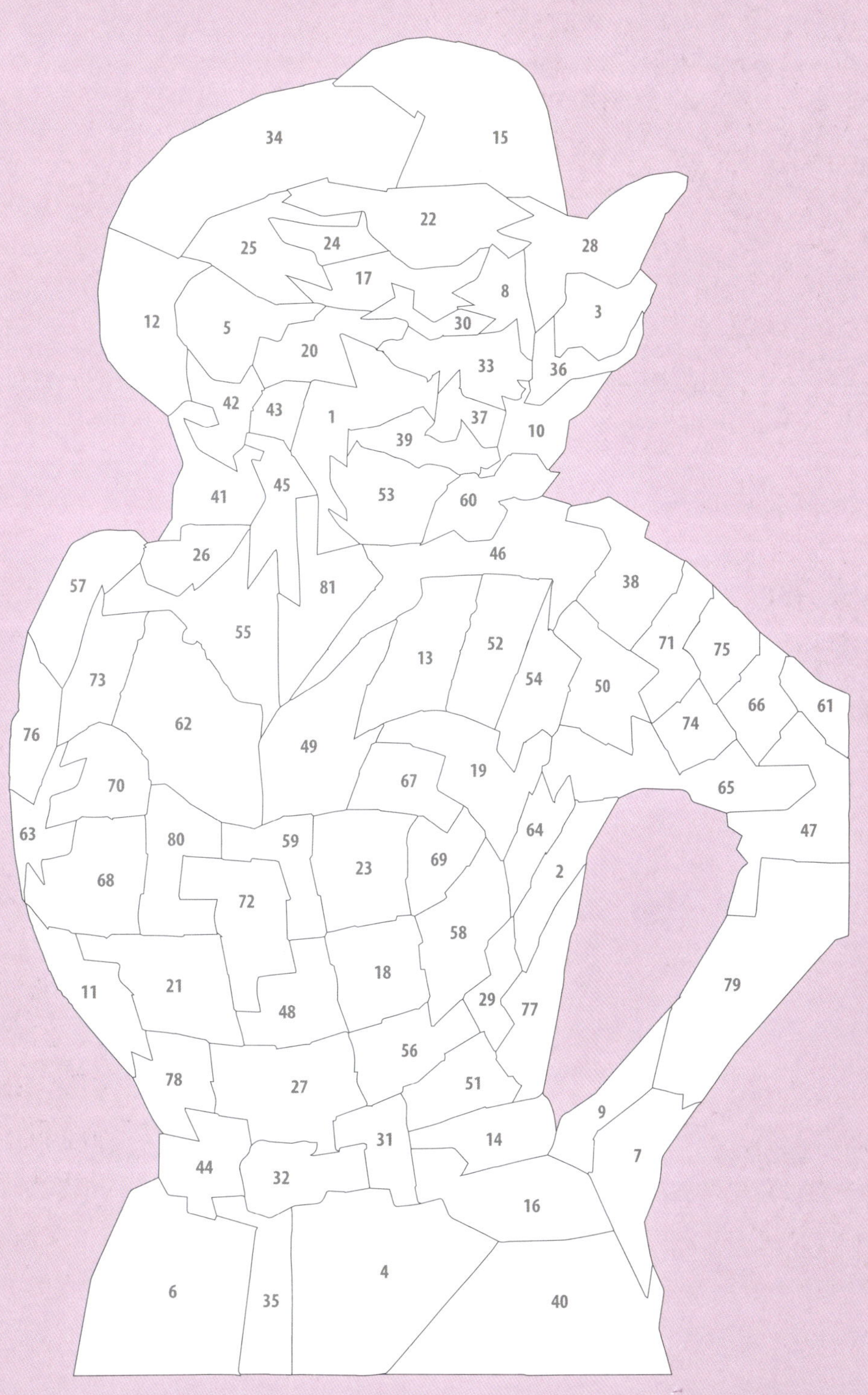

DOLLY PARTON

Dolly Rebecca Parton has captivated hearts worldwide with her remarkable journey from humble beginnings to unparalleled stardom. Born on January 19, 1946, Dolly was the fourth of twelve children raised by her parents, Robert Lee Parton and Avie Lee Caroline Owens. Her career has spanned over five decades, starting from 1956, and she has sold more than 100 million records worldwide.

Dolly Details

Family:
Robert and Avie Lee Parton (parents),
11 brothers and sisters

Hometown:
Sevierville, Tennessee

Spouse:
Carl Dean
(married for over 50 years)

Favorite Foods:
Banana pudding, chicken and dumplings,
roast pork

Musical Influences:
Rose Maddox, Kitty Wells,
Brenda Lee, Patsy Cline

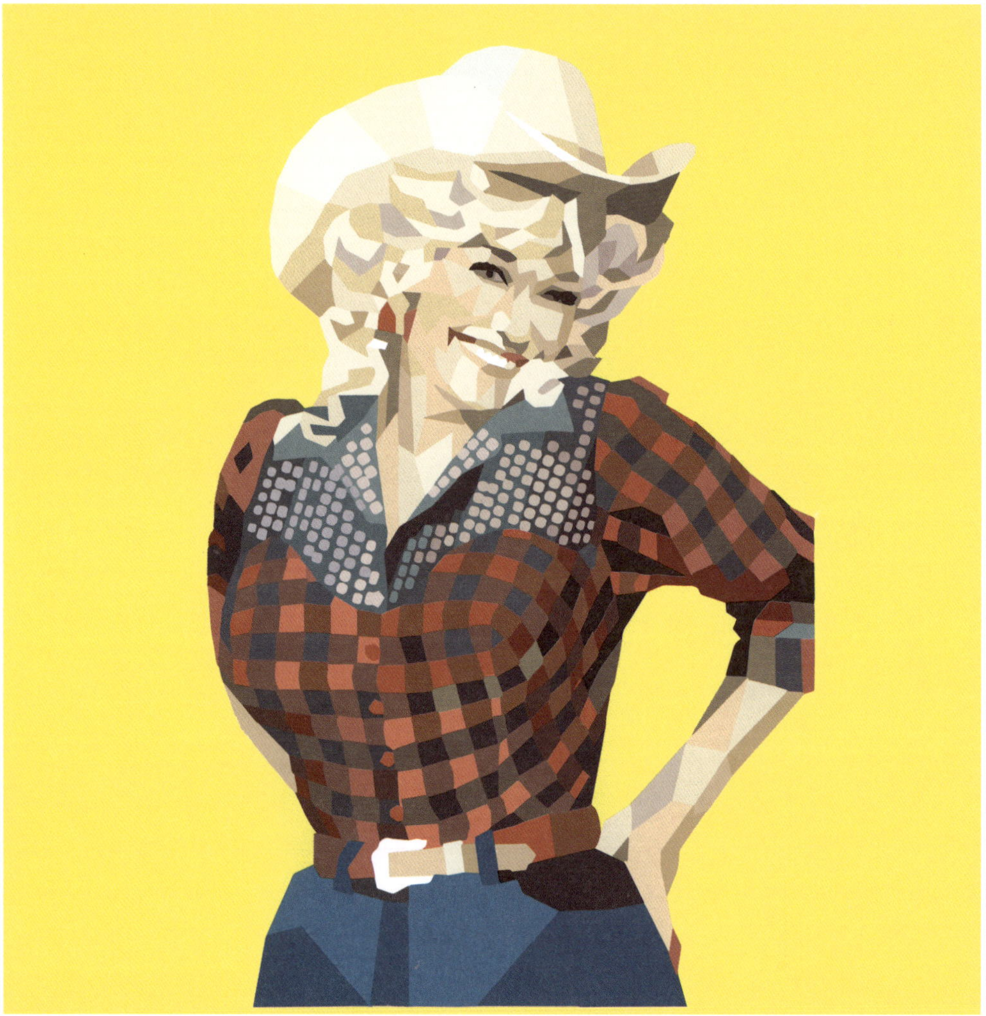

"If you don't like the road you're walking, start paving another one."

—Dolly Parton

RISING STAR

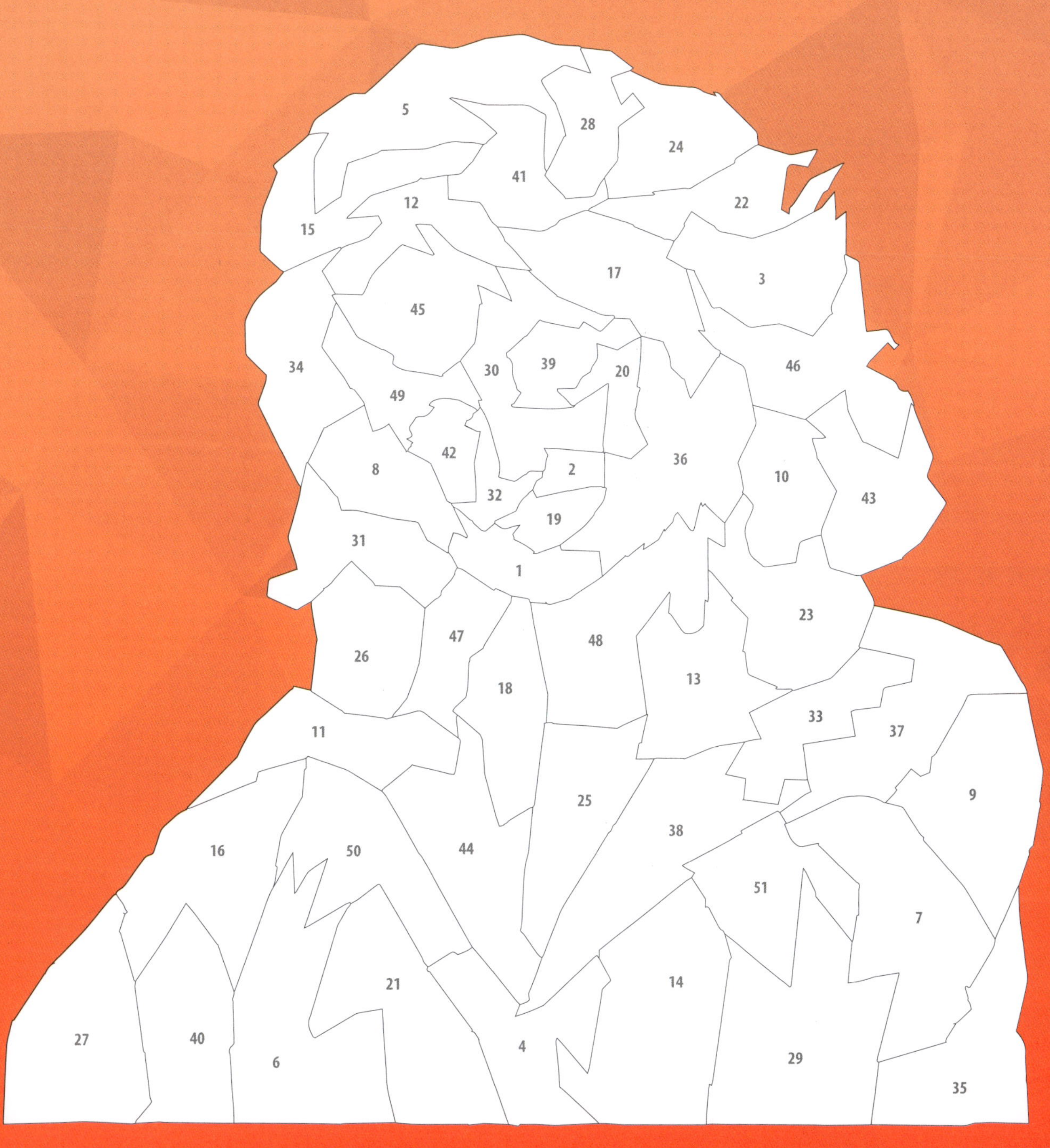

5
28
24
41
12
22
15
17
3
45
34
30
39
20
46
49
42
36
8
2
10
43
32
19
31
1
23
47
48
26
18
13
33
11
37
25
9
38
16
50
44
51
7
21
14
27
40
6
4
29
35

RISING STAR

Dolly's big break came when she joined the renowned *Porter Wagoner Show* in 1967, where her talent quickly overshadowed her mentor's. With a string of chart-topping hits, Dolly seamlessly blended country and pop, broadening the genre's appeal and paving the way for future crossover artists. Her partnership with Porter Wagoner lasted for seven years, during which they recorded several duets and had a successful television show.

Dolly Details

Show Information:
The Porter Wagoner Show, a musical variety show

First Dolly Appearance:
September, 1967

Duets:
"Say Forever You'll Be Mine"
"Just Someone I Used to Know"
"Making Plans"
"Please Don't Stop Loving Me"

Time Period:
Seven years— from 1967–1974

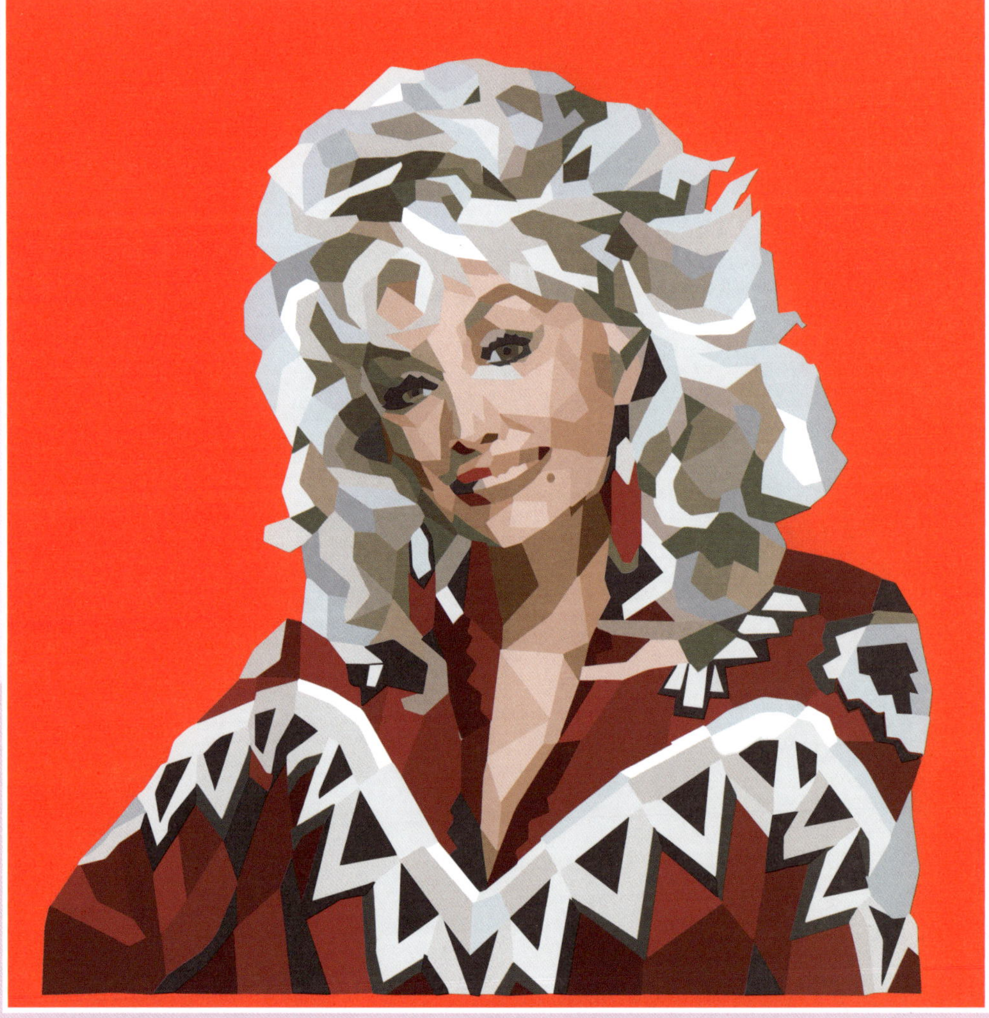

Fun Fact:

Dolly wrote "I Will Always Love You" as a special goodbye to Porter when she left the show.

MUSICAL LEGACY

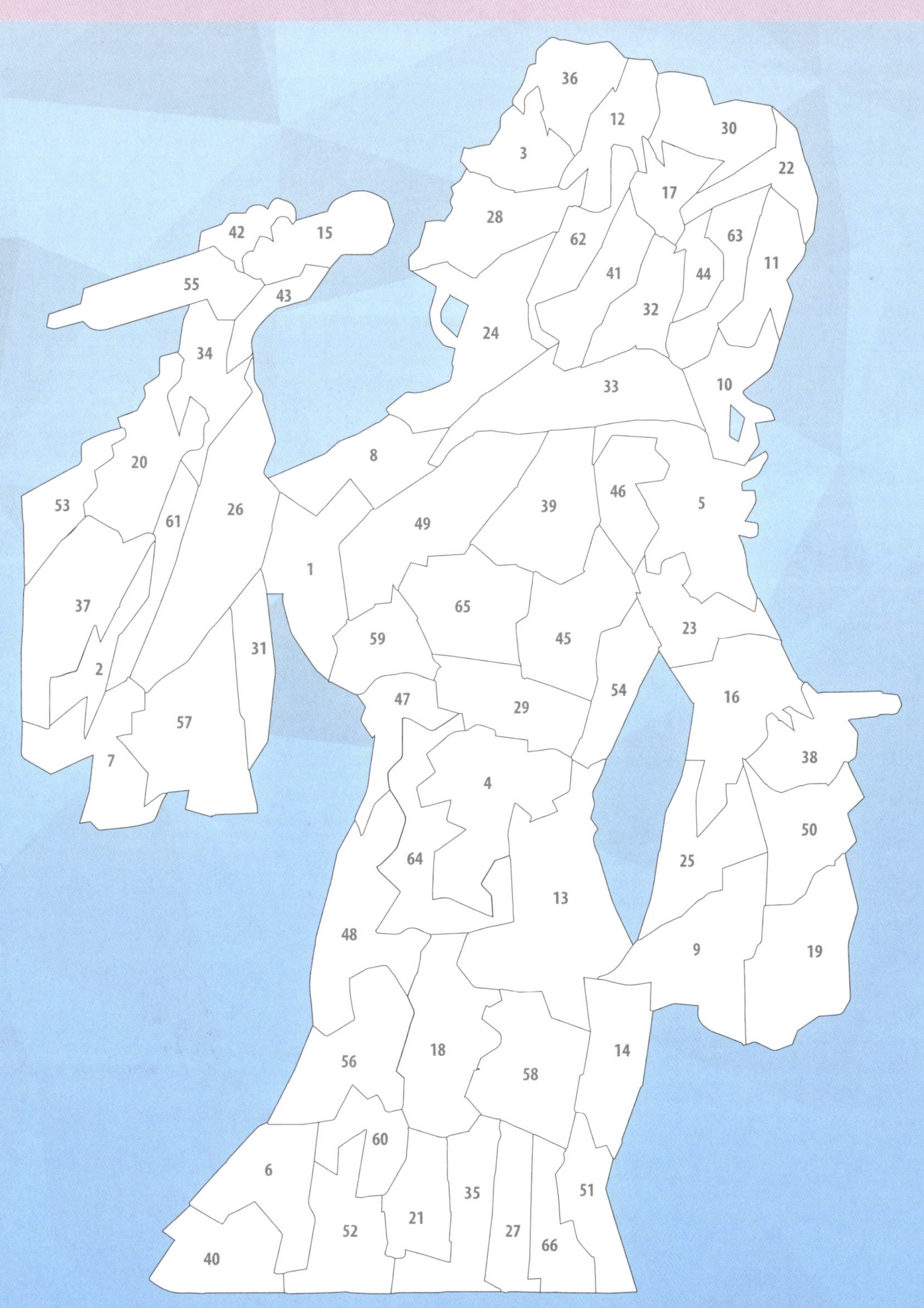

MUSICAL LEGACY

Dolly's musical legacy is unparalleled, with 25 number-one singles on the *Billboard* country charts and over 40 top-10 country albums. She's topped the country, pop, and adult contemporary charts simultaneously, been inducted in the Country Music Hall of Fame, and the Rock & Roll Hall of Fame. It's safe to say she's legendary.

Dolly Details

Genres:
Country, Gospel, Bluegrass, Pop, Rock

Hit Songs:
"Jolene," "I Will Always Love You," "9 to 5," "Here You Come Again," "The Bargain Store"

Hit Albums:
9 to 5 and Odd Jobs, Little Sparrow, Coat of Many Colors, The Grass Is Blue, My Tennessee Mountain Home

Awards:
11 Grammy awards, 9 CMA awards, 10 ACM awards

National Medal of Arts (2005), Kennedy Center Honors (2006)

Hall of Fame Inductions:
Nashville Songwriters Hall of Fame (1986), Country Music Hall of Fame (1999), Gospel Music Hall of Fame (2009), Rock & Roll Hall of Fame (2022)

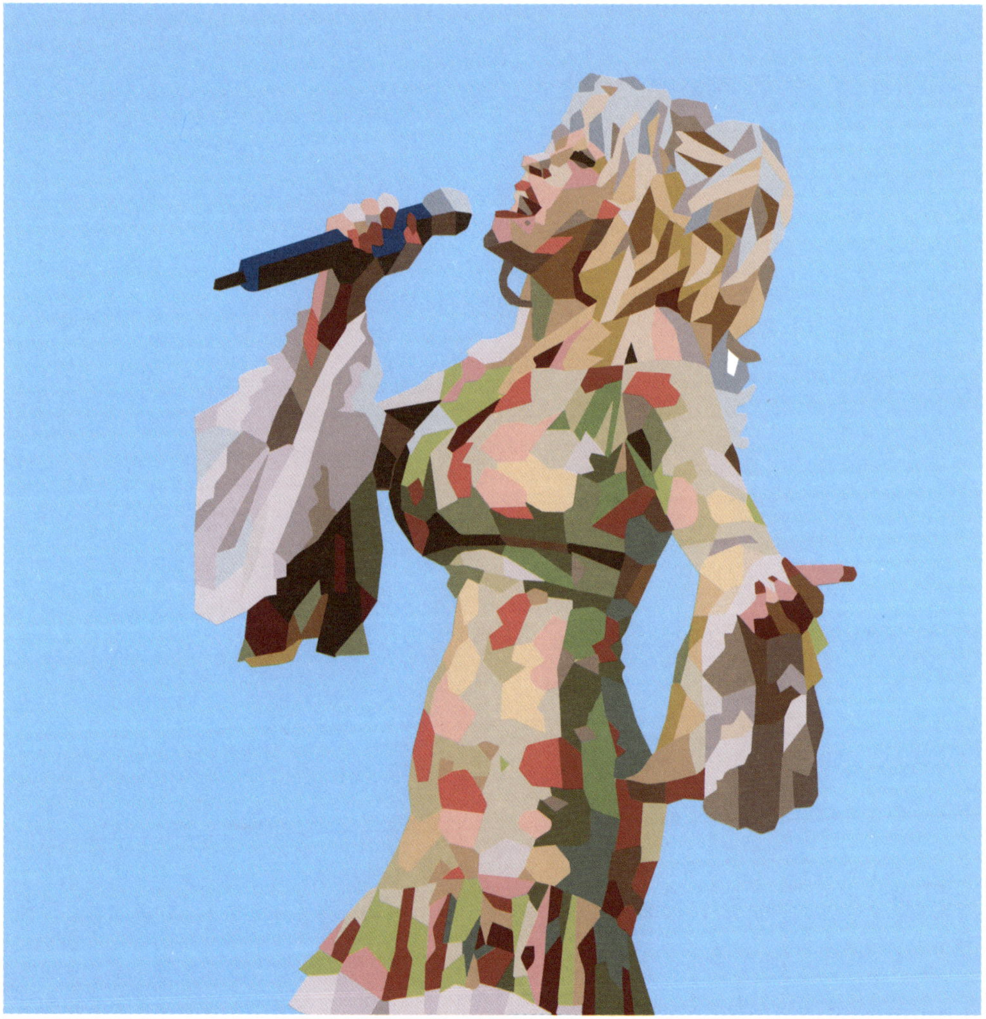

"It's hard to be a diamond in a rhinestone world."

—Dolly Parton

"JOLENE"

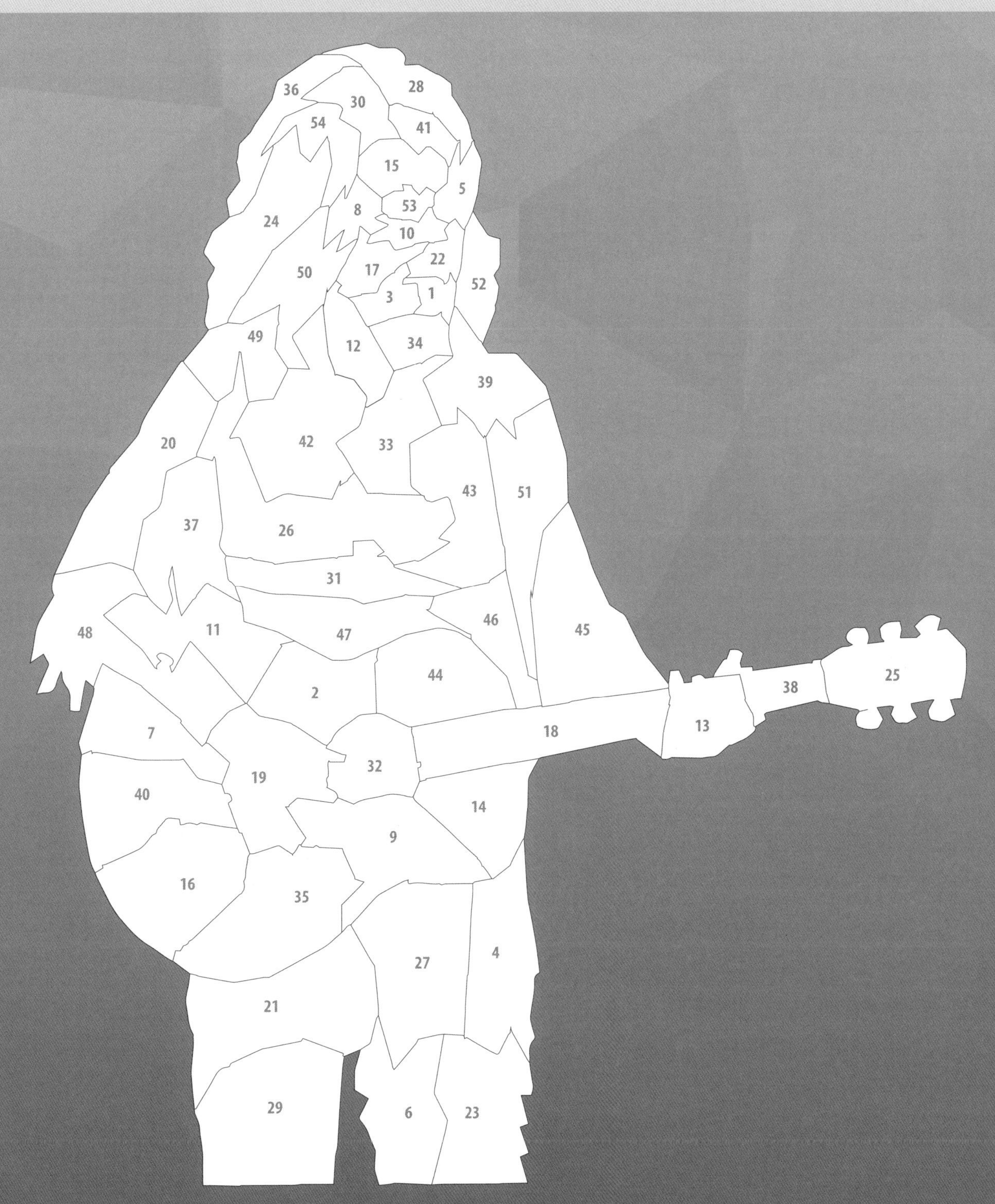

36
30
28
54
41
15
5
53
8
24
10
22
17
50
52
3
1
49
12
34
39
20
42
33
43
51
37
26
31
46
45
48
11
47
44
25
38
2
18
13
7
32
19
40
14
9
16
35
4
27
21
29
6
23

"JOLENE"

Released in 1973 as a single from her album of the same name, "Jolene" tells the story of a woman confronting another woman who she believes is trying to steal her lover. The song became an instant classic, reaching number one on the country charts and selling over 20 million copies worldwide. Dolly has revealed that the song was inspired by a real-life encounter with a bank teller who flirted with her husband, Carl Dean.

Dolly Details

Genre:
Country

Album:
Jolene

Dates:
May 22, 1973 (recorded)

October 15, 1973 (released)

Accolades:
Grammy Hall of Fame (2014),
Grammy award for Best Country Duo/Group Performance with Pentatonix (2017)

Inspirations:
Real-life encounter at a bank,
seeing a young girl in the crowd with red hair and green eyes named Jolene

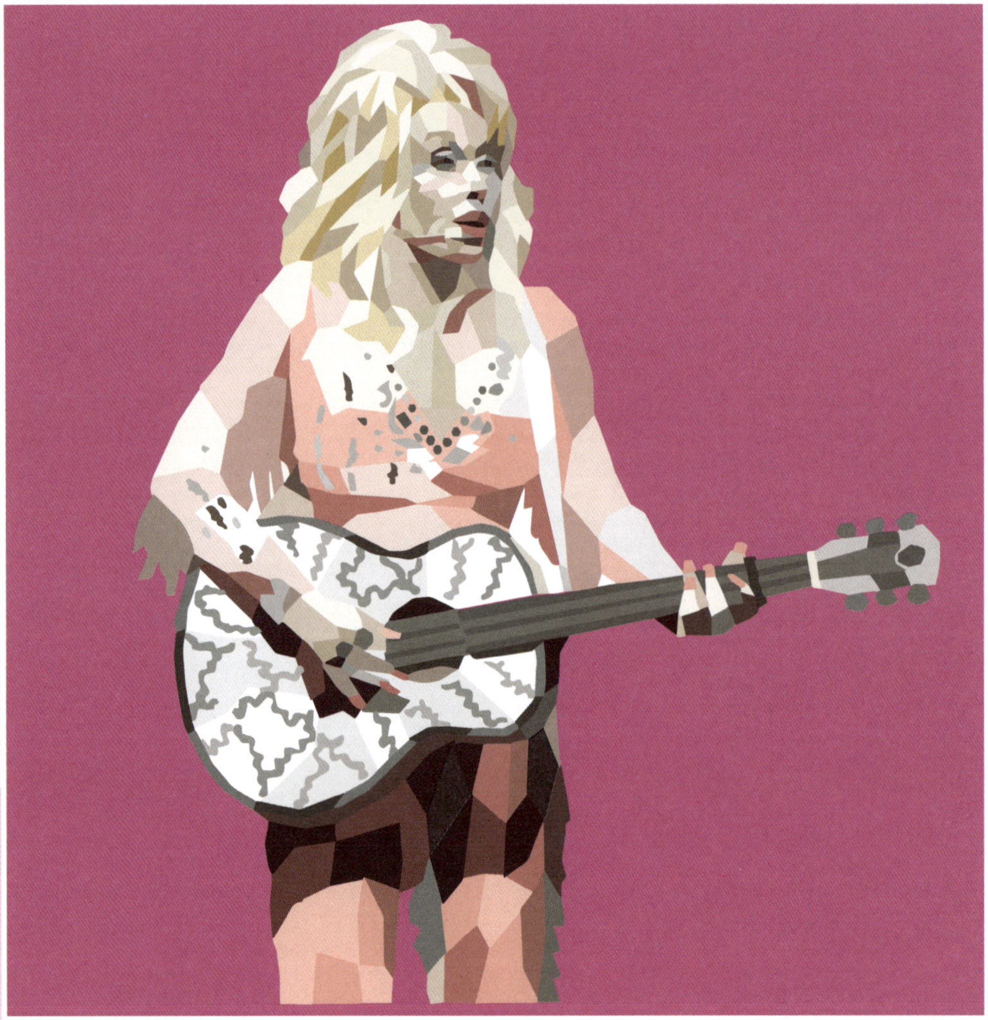

Fun Fact:

"Jolene" has been covered by many artists, including Miley Cyrus, Beyoncé, The White Stripes, Pentatonix, and Lil Nas X!

"I WILL ALWAYS LOVE YOU"

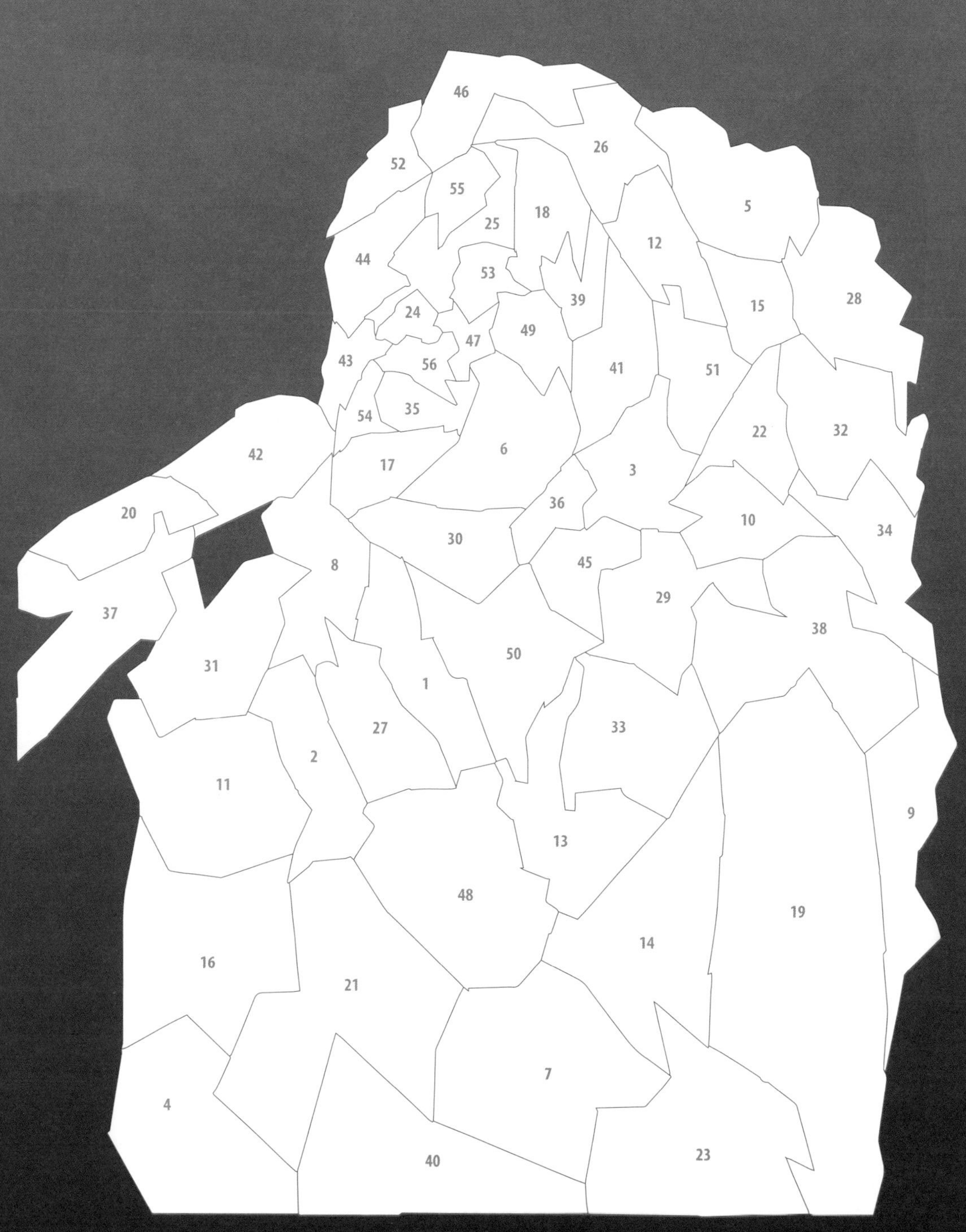

"I WILL ALWAYS LOVE YOU"

Originally written as a farewell to her mentor and duet partner, Porter Wagoner, when she decided to leave his show and pursue a solo career, "I Will Always Love You" became one of Dolly's signature songs. Released in 1974, the song reached number one on the country charts and has sold over 20 million copies worldwide. The song gained even more popularity when Whitney Houston covered it for the 1992 film *The Bodyguard*, which became one of the best-selling singles of all time, with over 20 million copies sold.

Dolly Details

Genre:
Country

Album:
Jolene

Dates:
June 12, 1973 (recorded)

March 11, 1974 (released)

Accolades:
Number one on *Billboard*'s country chart, CMA awards: Female Vocalist of the Year (1975)

Whitney Houston
Whitney Houston's version was recorded for *The Bodyguard* in 1992, turning the song into a global sensation. Whitney won the Grammy awards for Record of the Year and Best Pop Vocal Performance, Female in 1994.

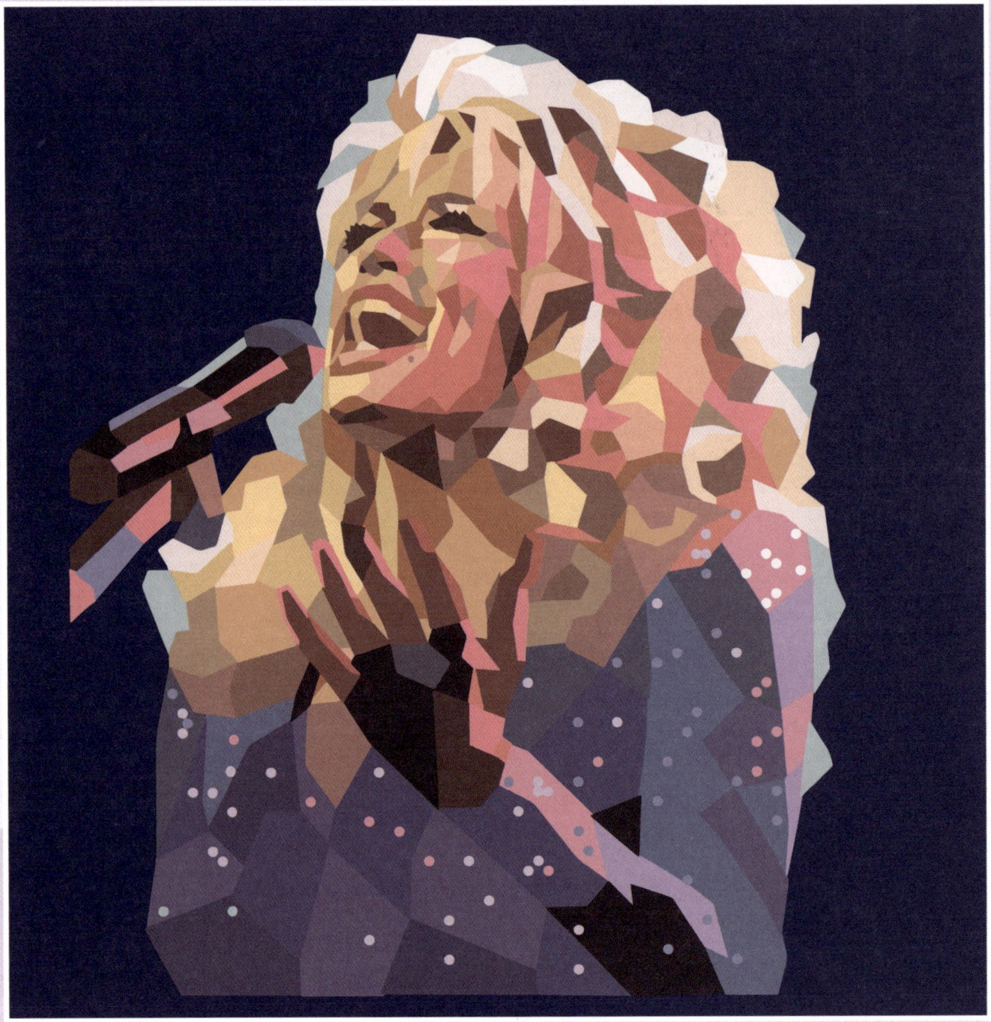

Fun Fact:

Dolly famously declined Elvis Presley's request to record the song first, because he wanted at least half the publishing credits!

ACTING CAREER

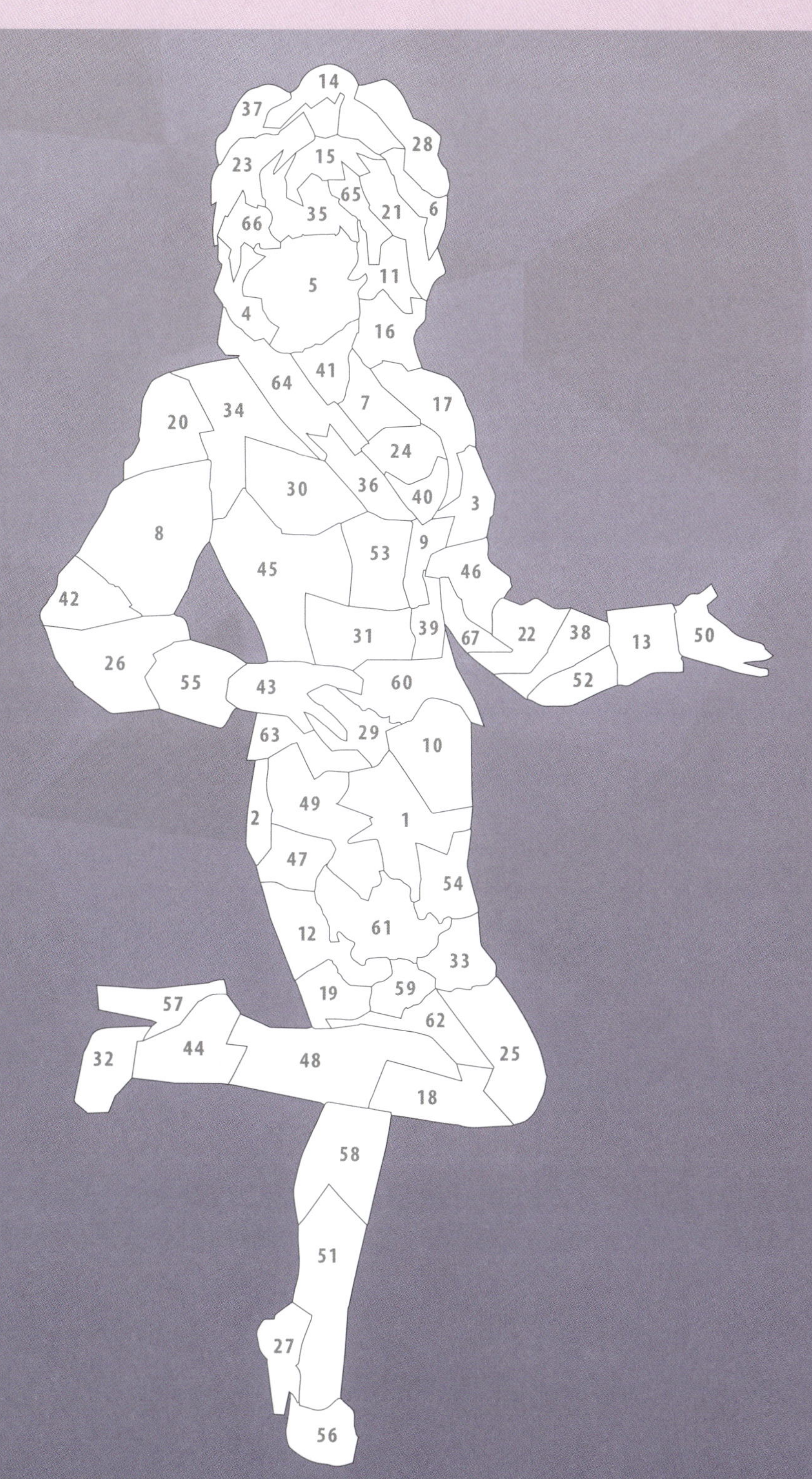

ACTING CAREER

In addition to her illustrious music career, Dolly has also made a name for herself as an actress, starring in several commercially successful films. Her charm, comedic timing, and versatility helped endear her films and television shows to people around the world for many years to come.

Dolly Details

Genre:
Comedy, musical, drama, romantic comedy

Movies:
9 to 5, *Rhinestone*, *Steel Magnolias*, *Straight Talk*, *The Beverly Hillbillies*

TV Shows:
The Porter Wagoner Show, *Dolly*

Accolades:
People's Choice Awards: Favorite Female Performer in a New TV Program (1988, for *Dolly*), Primetime Emmy Awards: Outstanding Television Movie (2021, for *Christmas on the Square*)

Songs for Film:
"9 to 5" from *9 to 5*

"Tennessee Homesick Blues" from *Rhinestone*

"Straight Talk" from *Straight Talk*

"Girl in the Movies" from *Dumplin'*

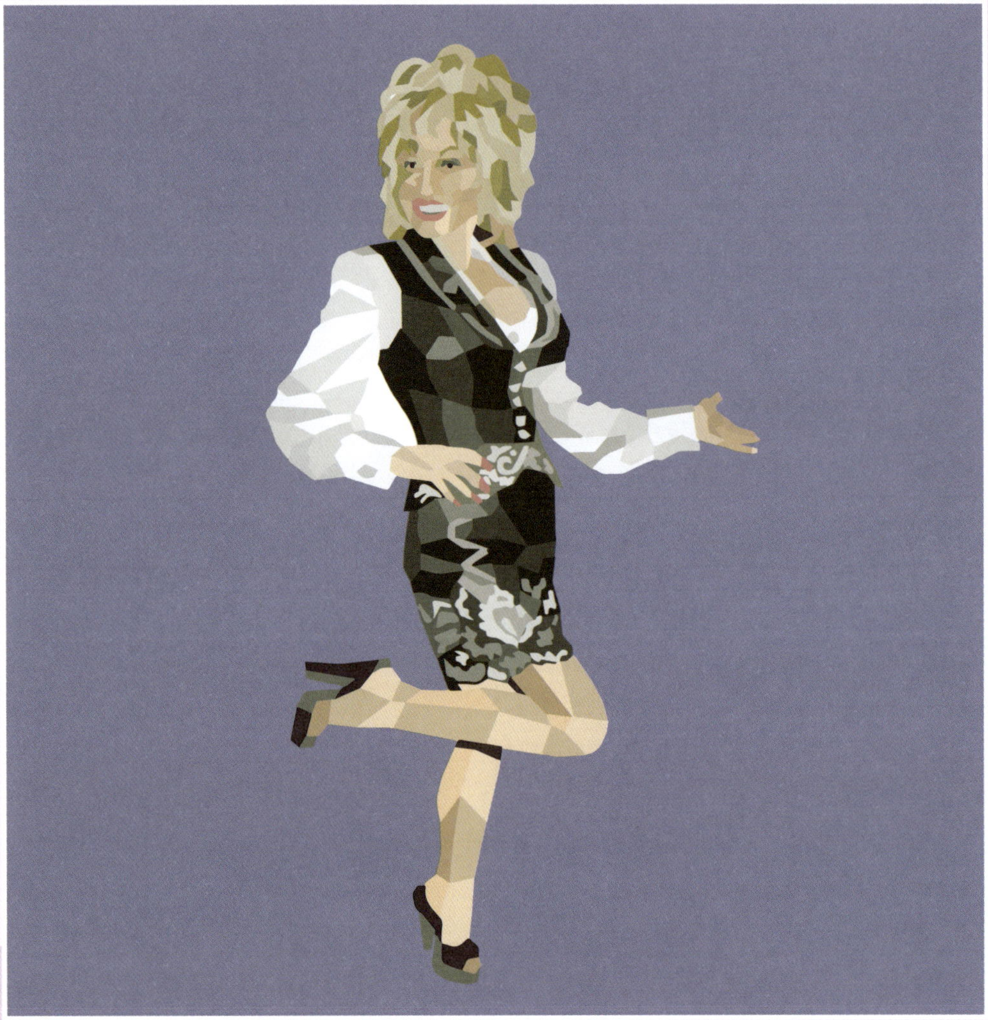

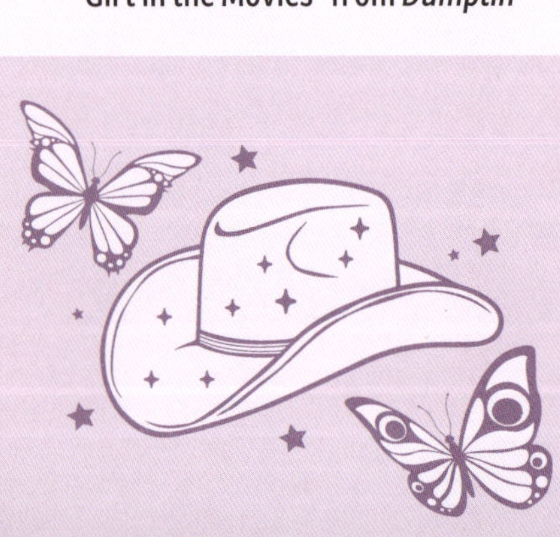

"I never tried quitting, and I never quit trying."

—Dolly Parton

9 TO 5

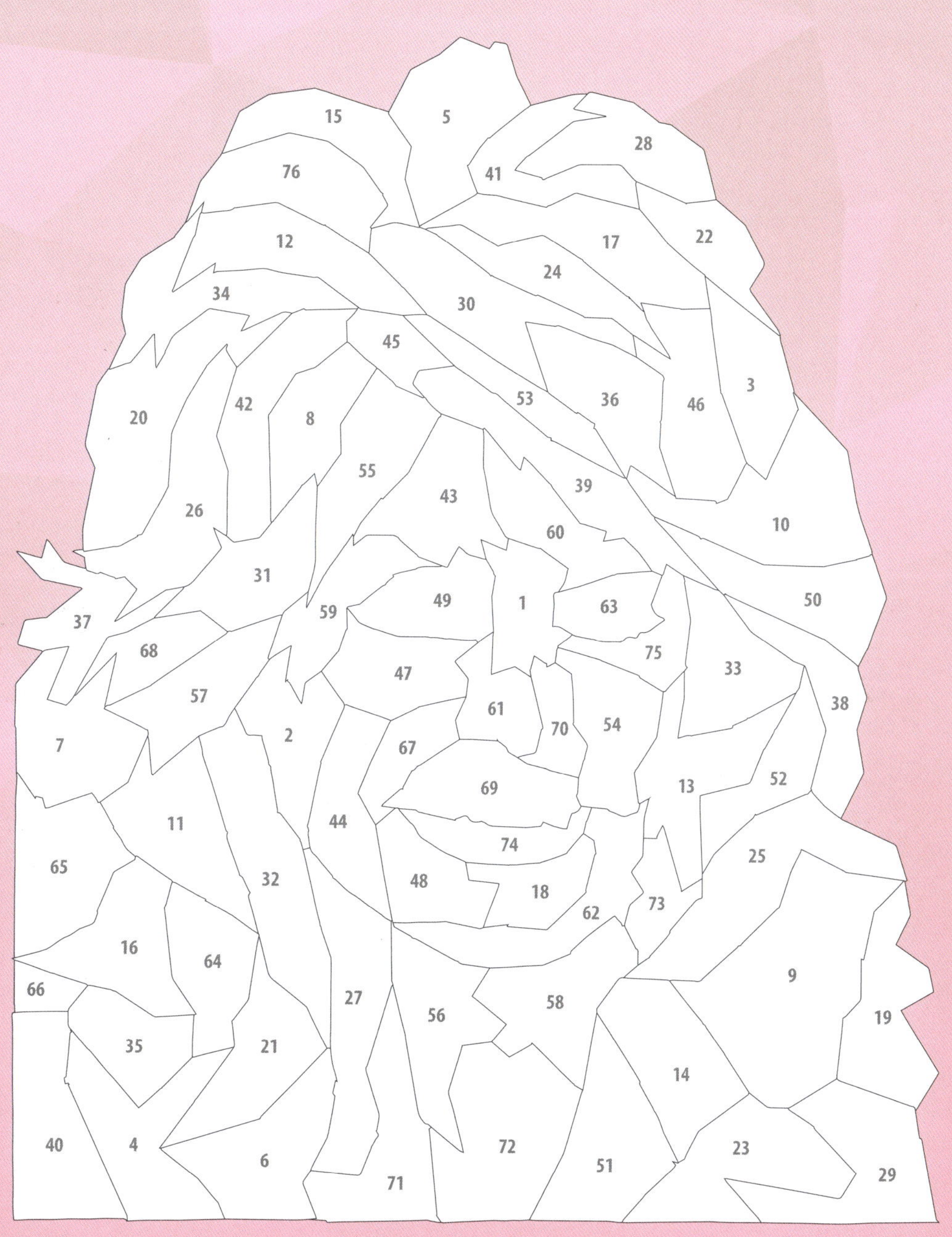

9 TO 5

In her film debut, Dolly starred in a comedy about three secretaries who take revenge on their sexist boss. The movie was a critical and commercial success, grossing over $100 million at the box office and receiving multiple Golden Globe and Academy Award nominations. Dolly's performance earned her a Golden Globe nomination as well!

Dolly Details

Genre:
Comedy

Character:
Doralee Rhodes

Costars:
Jane Fonda, Lily Tomlin, Dabney Coleman

Accolades:
Grammy Awards: Best Country Vocal Performance, Female and Best Country Song (1980, for "9 to 5"), nominations at Academy Awards and Golden Globes

Other Versions:
TV series (1982-3, 1986-8)

Broadway musical (2009)

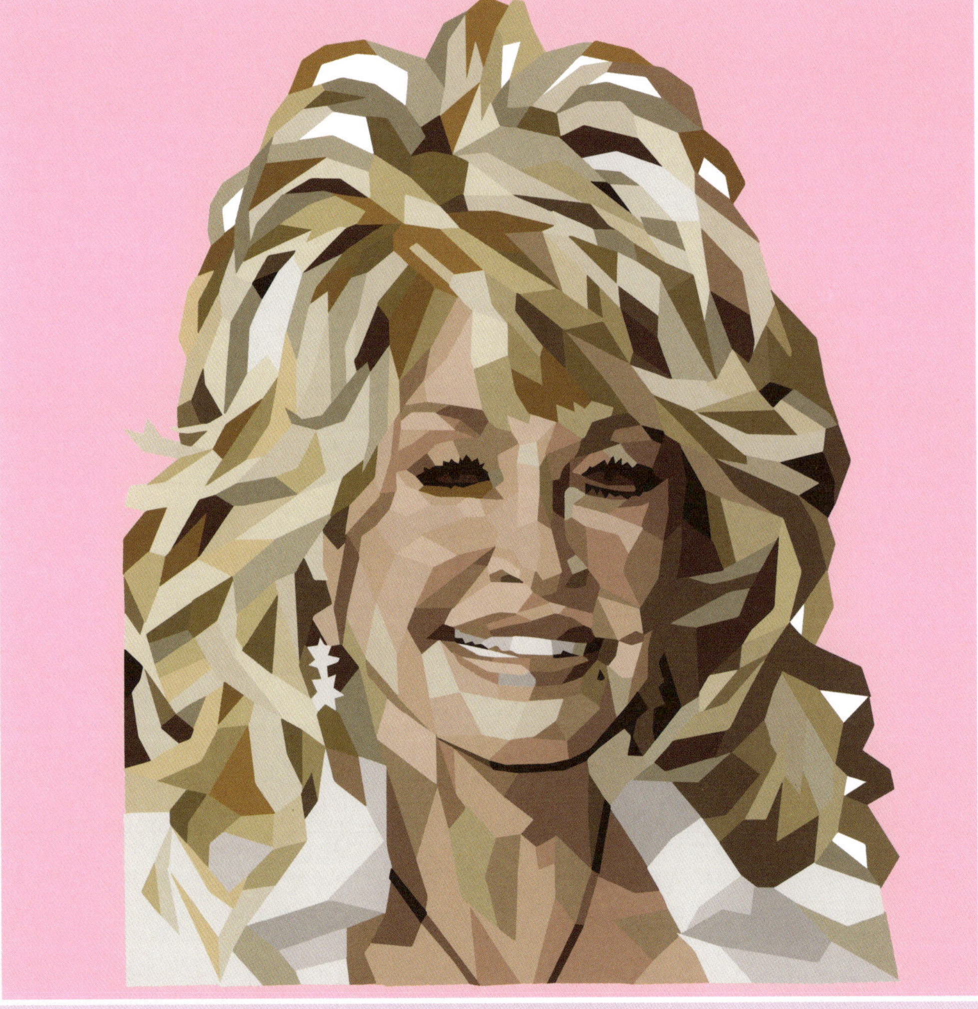

Fun Fact:

In 2024, Jennifer Anniston announced that she is working on a *9 to 5* reboot, with Dolly in full support!

STEEL MAGNOLIAS

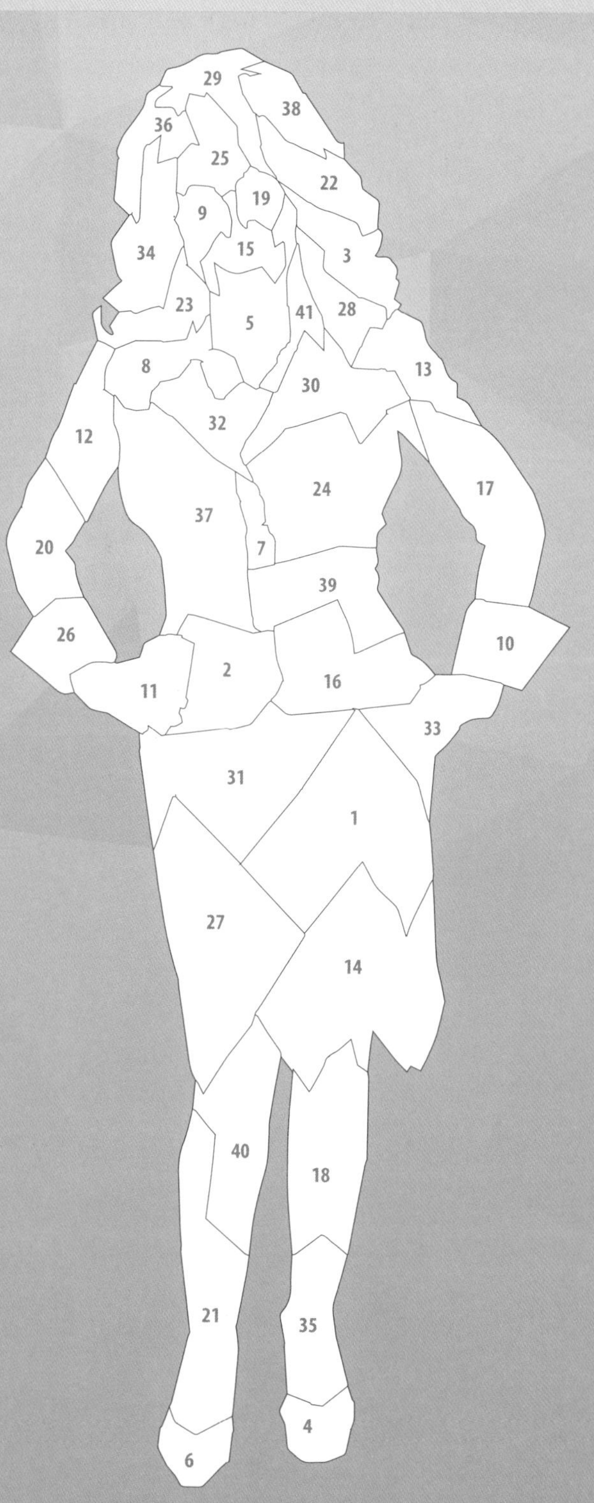

STEEL MAGNOLIAS

In this beloved drama, Dolly played the role of a beauty salon owner in a small Louisiana town. The film boasted an all-star cast and was a critical and commercial success. The film received multiple Academy Award and Golden Globe nominations, and Dolly's performance earned widespread acclaim.

Dolly Details

Genre:
Comedy-drama

Character:
Truvy Jones

Costars:
Sally Field, Shirley MacLaine, Daryl Hannah, Olympia Dukakis, Julia Roberts

Accolades:
People's Choice Awards: Favorite Dramatic Motion Picture (1990), nominations at the Golden Globes, Academy Awards

Other Versions:
Broadway play (1987)

TV pilot (1990)

Remake on Lifetime (2012)

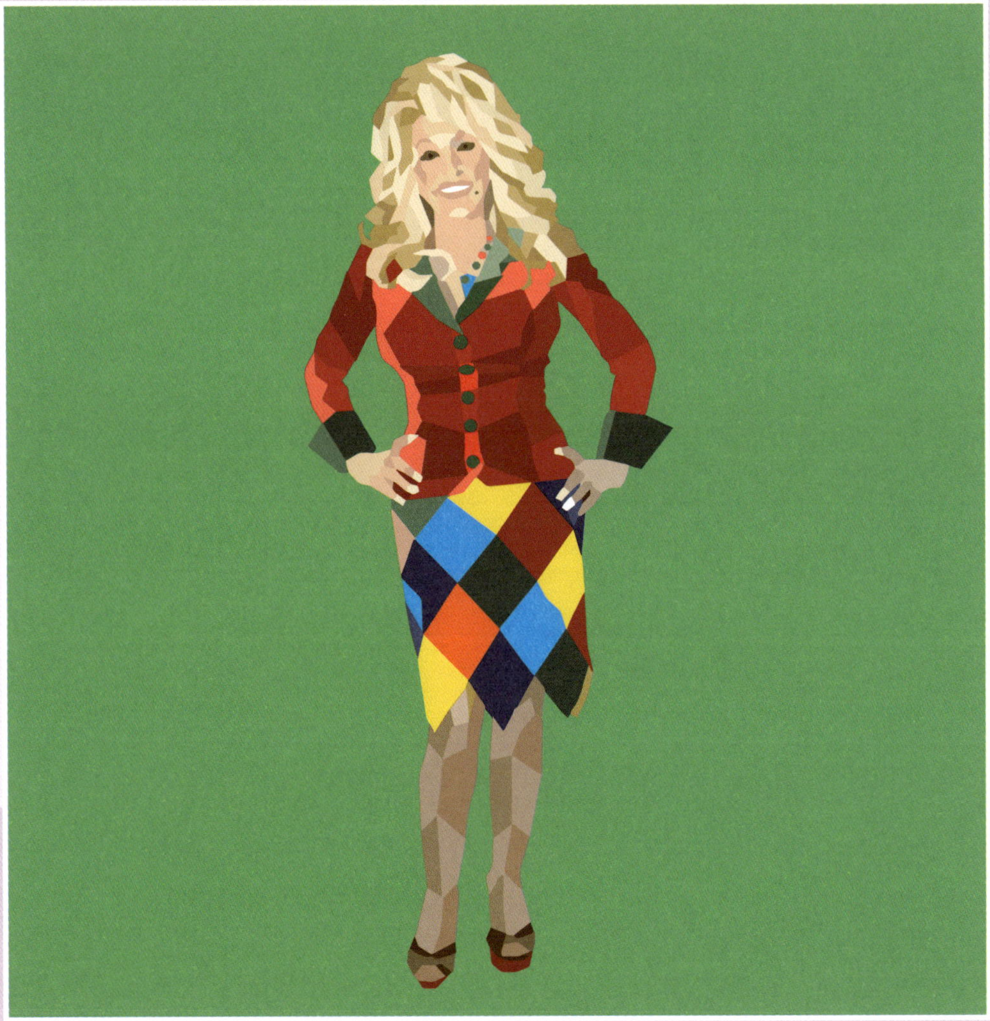

Fun Fact:

While filming, the director, Herbert Ross, once asked Dolly Parton if she knew how to act. She quickly replied, "No, but it's your job to make me look like I can!"

GOOD DEEDS

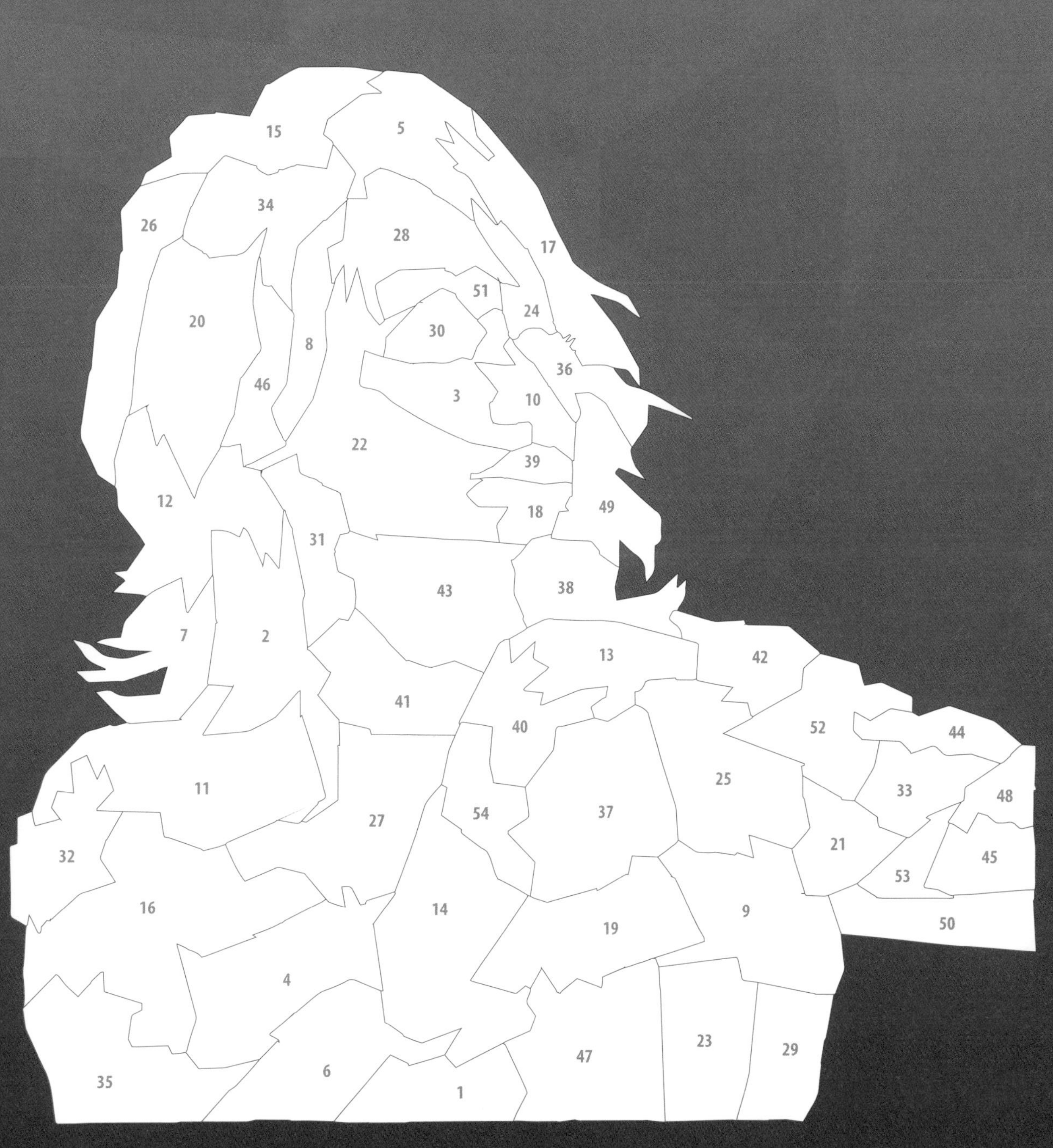

15
5
34
26
28
17
51
24
20
30
8
36
46
3
10
22
39
12
49
18
31
38
43
7
2
13
42
41
40
52
44
25
33
48
11
37
54
27
21
32
45
53
16
14
9
19
50
4
23
29
47
6
35
1

GOOD DEEDS

Beyond her artistic endeavors, Dolly's philanthropic efforts have made a significant impact on countless lives. In 1988, Dolly created the Dollywood Foundation with the goal of inspiring the students in Sevier County, Tennessee to stay in school. Thanks to Dolly, the dropout rate lowered to 6% that year. And it was only the beginning of Dolly's good deeds.

Dolly Details

Dollywood®:
Provides employment opportunities for the local community, offers 100% tuition, fee, and book coverage for employees

Dolly's Imagination Library®:
Has gifted over 224 million books to children worldwide

The Dolly Parton Scholarship:
An annual $15,000 college scholarship gifted to Sevier County high-school seniors

Middle Tennessee Flood Relief:
Raised $700,000 to help residents effected by the Middle Tennessee flooding in 2021

Carnegie Medal of Philanthropy:
Given to Dolly Parton in 2022

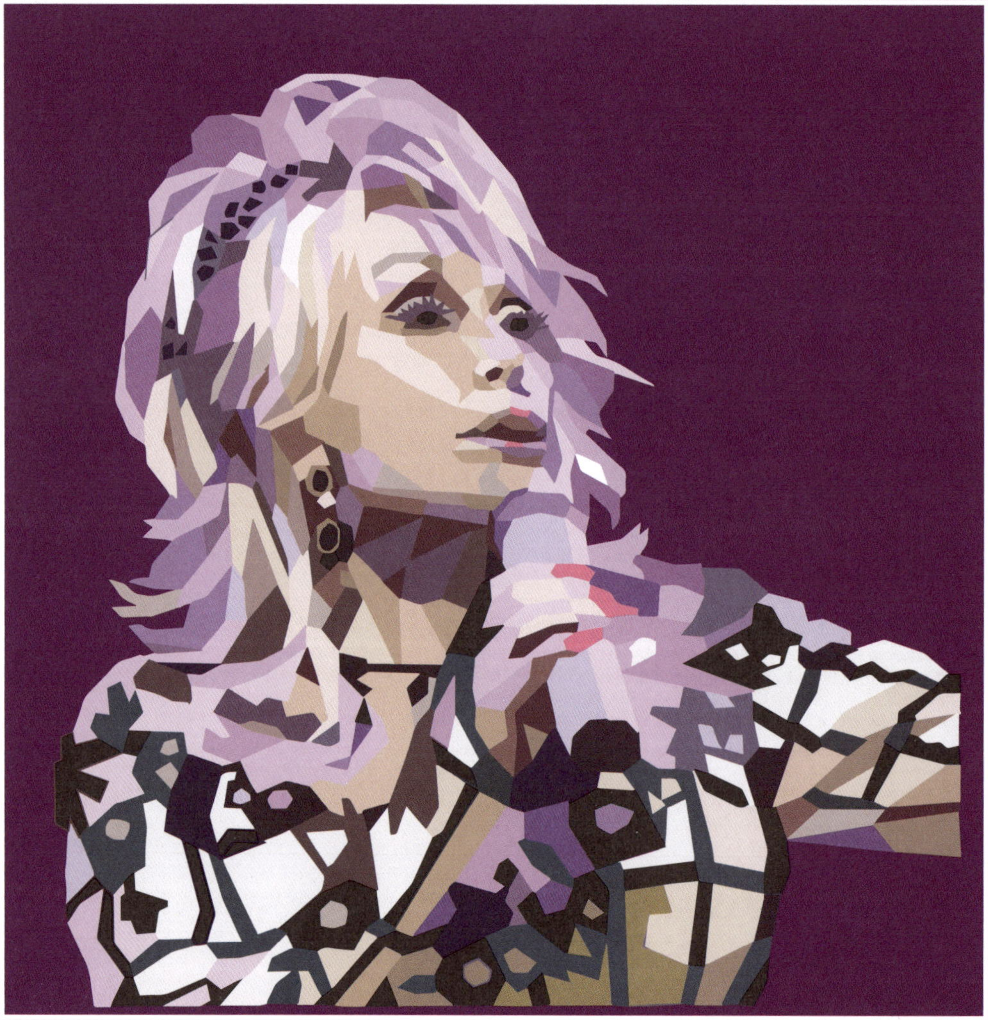

"I always just thought, if you see somebody without a smile, give 'em yours!"

—Dolly Parton

DOLLYWOOD®

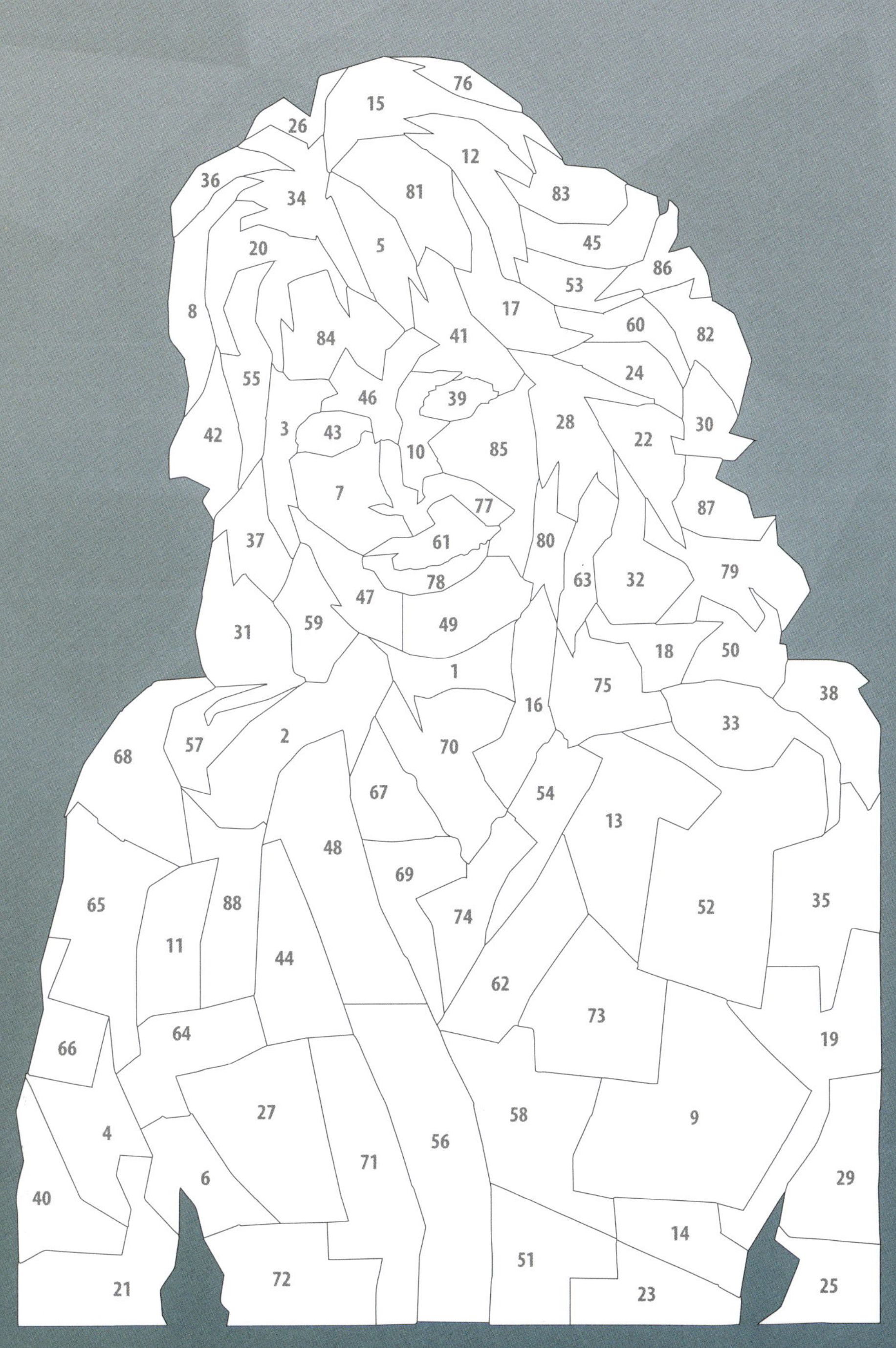

DOLLYWOOD®

In 1986, Dolly founded the Dollywood theme park in Pigeon Forge, Tennessee, which attracts millions of visitors annually and provides employment opportunities and tuition coverage for the local community. Dolly's goal was to provide an escape for families who needed a getaway. Dolly herself has also made countless appearances at Dollywood over the years, often performing live shows and greeting fans throughout the park. Her presence and personal touch have helped make Dollywood a truly unique and beloved destination for millions of visitors from around the world.

Dolly Details

Location:
Pigeon Forge, Tennessee

Attractions:
Roller coasters, water park, The Dolly Parton Experience

Live Entertainment:
Musical performances: country, bluegrass, Southern gospel, rock & roll, Appalachian artists

Accolades:
Golden Ticket Awards: Best Amusement Park (2023), Best Family Coaster (2023 for Big Bear Mountain), Best Kids' Area (2023), Best Guest Experience (2023)

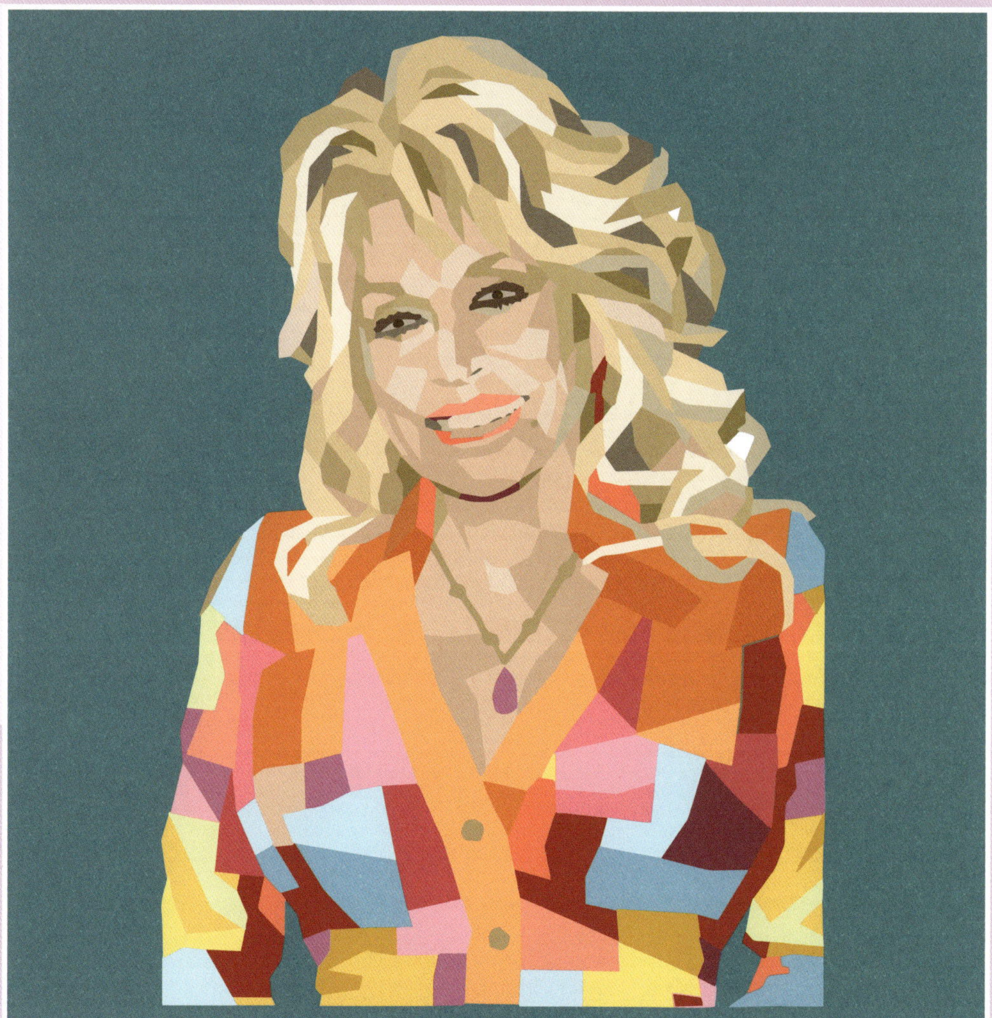

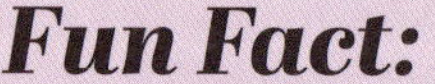

Fun Fact:

Even though she owns a theme park, Dolly is afraid of roller coasters and refuses to ride the rides!

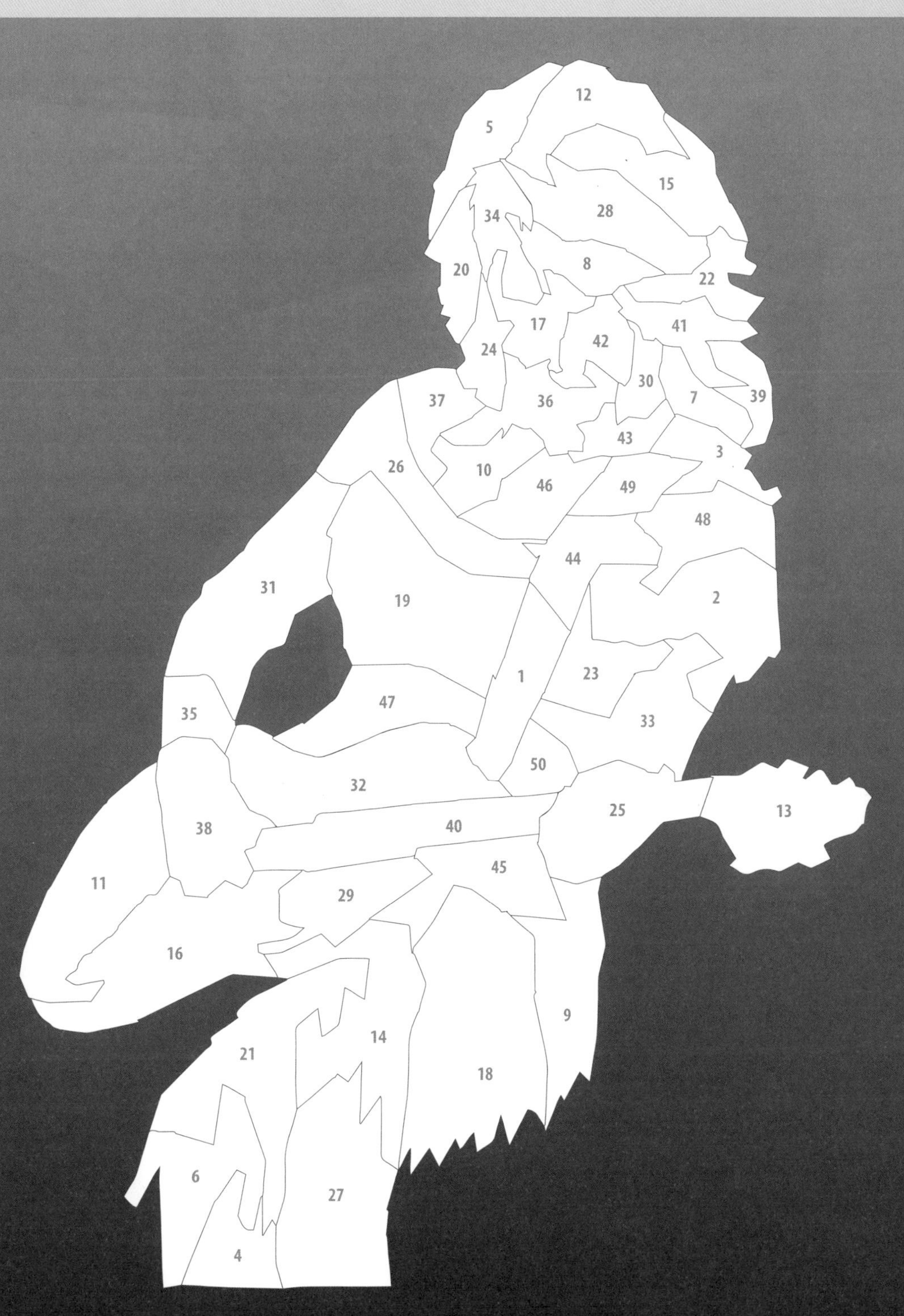
12
5
15
34
28
8
20
22
17
42
41
24
30
37
36
7
39
43
3
26
10
46
49
48
44
31
19
2
1
23
47
35
33
50
32
25
13
38
40
45
11
29
16
9
14
21
18
6
27
4

IMAGINATION LIBRARY®

In 1995, Dolly created the Imagination Library, a book-gifting program that send free books to children until they are five years old! The Imagination Library has gifted over 224 million books to children worldwide, promoting literacy and a love for reading. The program, which began in her hometown, Sevier County, Tennessee, now reaches children in five countries and has been praised for its impact on early childhood education.

Dolly Details

Countries:
USA, Canada, UK, Australia, Republic of Ireland

Inspiration:
A tribute to her father, who was unable to read

Accolades:
Library of Congress Literacy Awards: $150K
David M. Rubenstein Prize (2021),
National Educational Education Association Awards: Friends of Education Award (2022),
Carnegie Medal of Philanthropy Award (2022)

Books Gifted:
Two million books per month

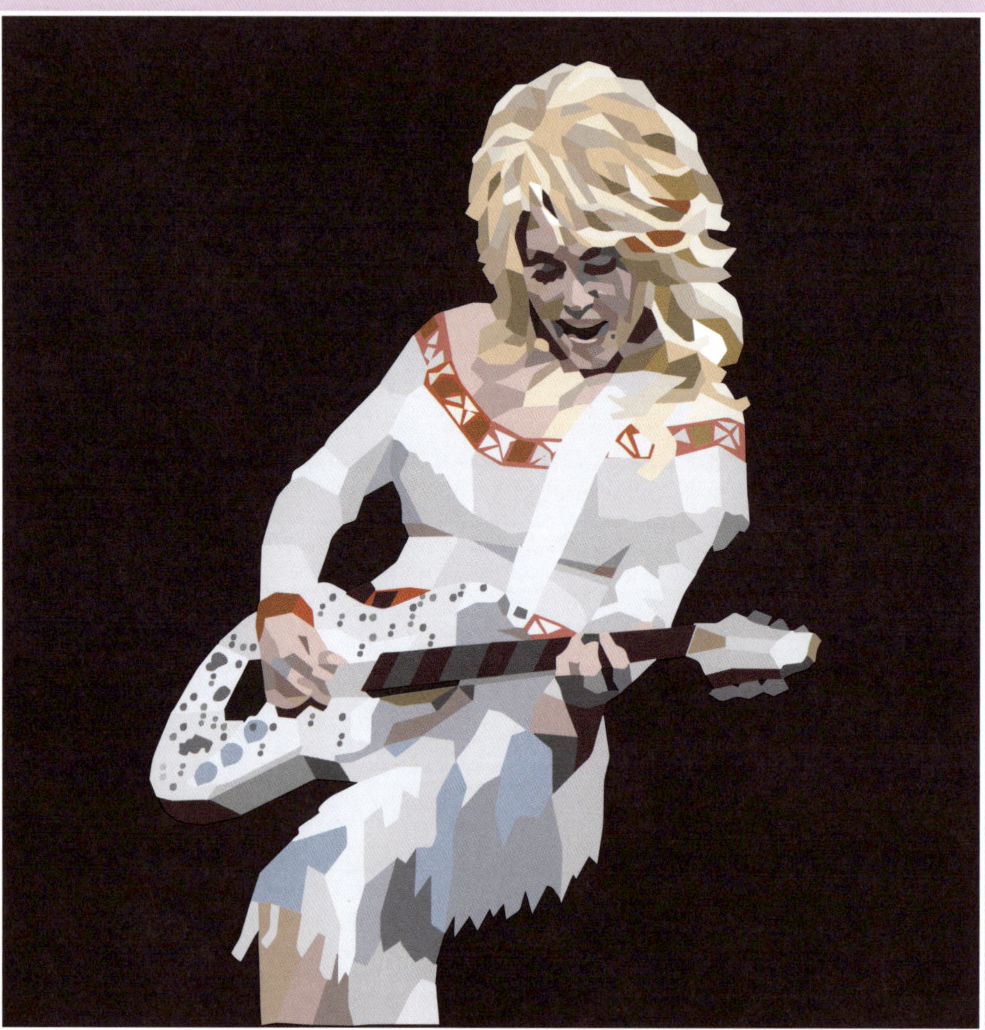

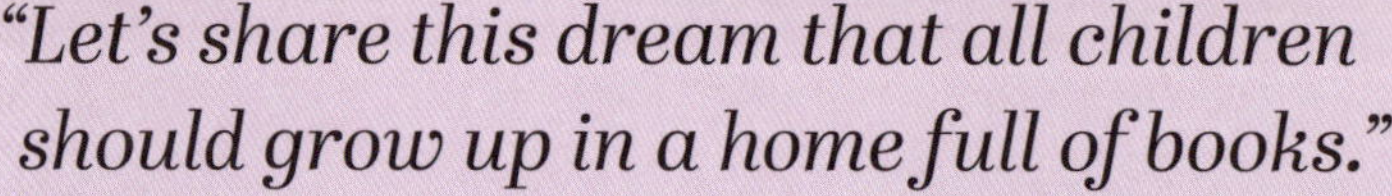

AN INSPIRATION TO ALL

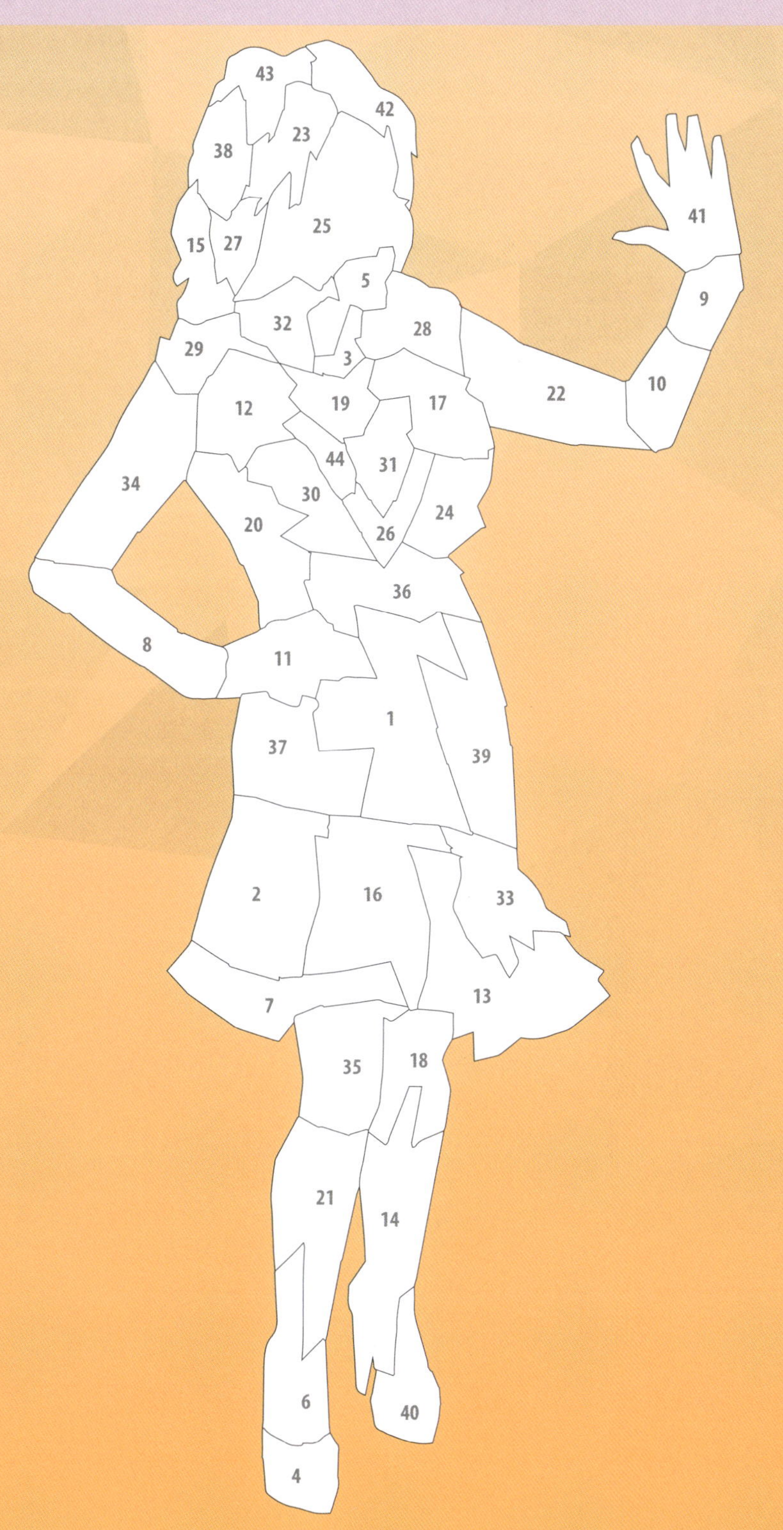

AN INSPIRATION TO ALL

Dolly Parton's journey is a testament to the power of perseverance, talent, and unwavering faith. Her life story serves as a beacon of hope, reminding everyone that with determination and a willingness to embrace our dreams, anything is possible. Dolly's music, acting, and philanthropic endeavors have inspired generations, transcending boundaries, and touching the lives of millions worldwide.

Dolly Details

Challenges to Overcome:
Growing up in poverty, lack of access to education and resources, overcoming stereotypes, navigating male-dominated country music scene

Fighting Back with Music:
Wrote "Coat of Many Colors," "Makin' Fun Ain't Funny" to promote self-acceptance and anti-bullying

The Butterfly:
Growing up, Dolly loved butterflies, because they symbolized freedom—being able to fly away. She incorporates butterflies everywhere now!

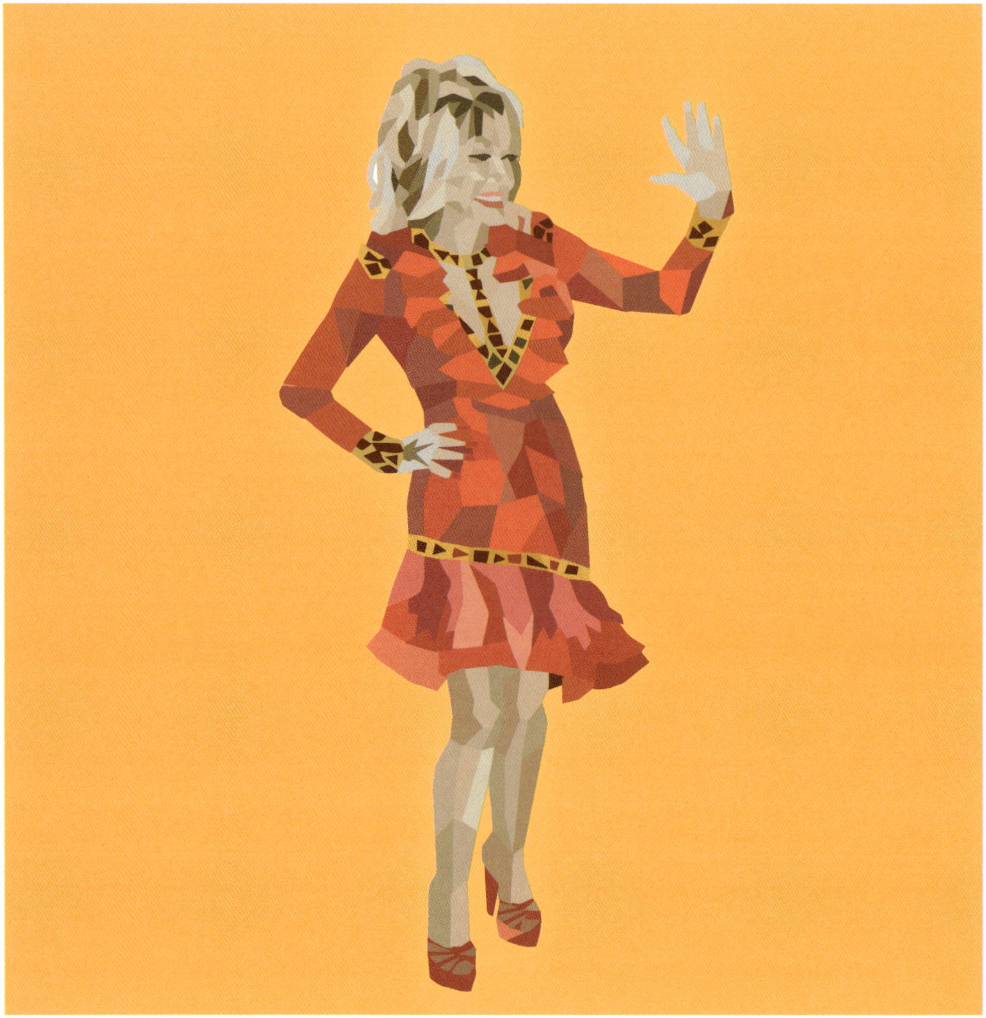

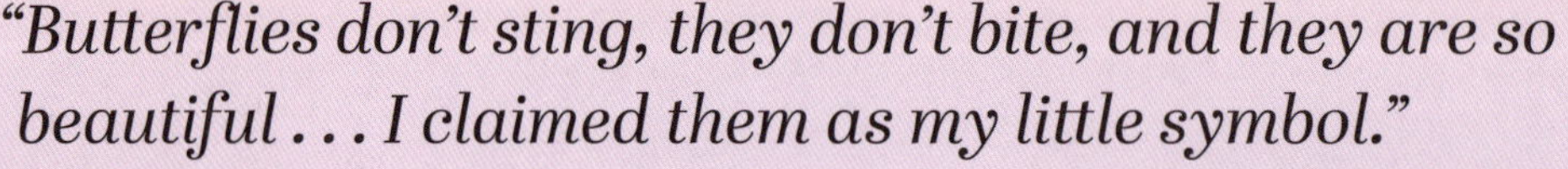

"Butterflies don't sting, they don't bite, and they are so beautiful . . . I claimed them as my little symbol."

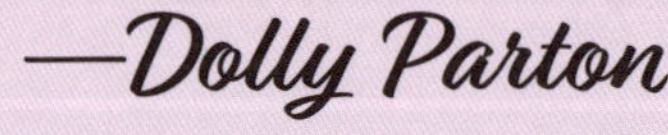

—Dolly Parton

Dolly's Top 10 Tracks

1. "Jolene" (1973)

One of Dolly's most iconic songs, "Jolene" is known for its haunting melody and captivating lyrics about a woman pleading with another not to take her man.

2. "I Will Always Love You" (1974)

This heartfelt ballad, written as a farewell to Porter Wagoner, became a massive hit for Dolly and was famously covered by Whitney Houston in 1992, bringing it international acclaim.

3. "9 to 5" (1980)

The title track for the film *9 to 5*, this song became an anthem for working women and a major crossover hit, reaching the top of both country and pop charts.

4. "Coat of Many Colors" (1971)

An autobiographical song that tells the story of Dolly's childhood, this track is beloved for its emotional depth and storytelling.

5. "Here You Come Again" (1977)

This song marked Dolly's successful crossover into pop music and became one of her biggest hits, showcasing her versatility as an artist.

6. "Islands in the Stream" (1983)

A duet with Kenny Rogers, this song topped the charts and became one of the most famous duets in country music history, blending country and pop influences.

7. "Tennessee Mountain Home" (1973)

This nostalgic track reflects Dolly's love for her Tennessee roots and her ability to paint vivid pictures through her lyrics.

8. "Love Is Like a Butterfly" (1974)

A gentle, uplifting song that became one of Dolly's signature tracks, known for its sweet melody and positive message.

9. "Why'd You Come in Here Lookin' Like That" (1989)

A catchy, upbeat track that became a major hit in the late 1980s, showcasing Dolly's fun and playful side.

10. "Two Doors Down" (1977)

A popular track from the album *Here You Come Again*, this song combines Dolly's storytelling with an infectious melody and upbeat rhythm.

STICKERS

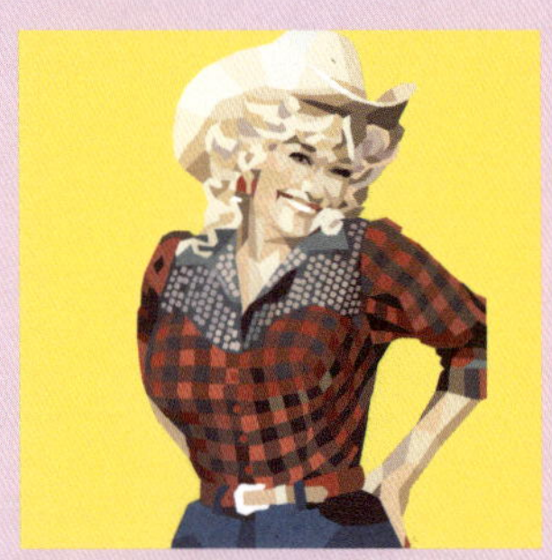
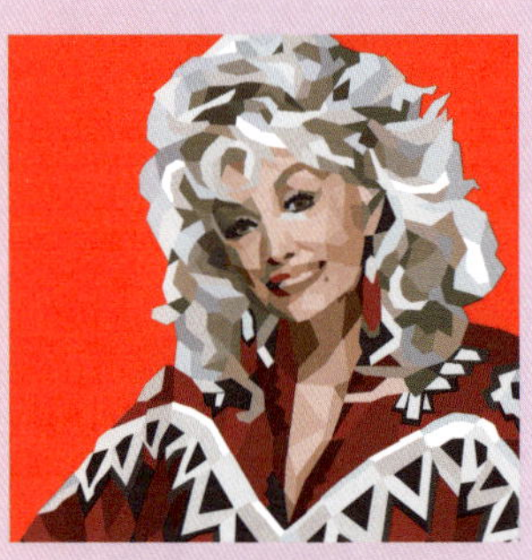
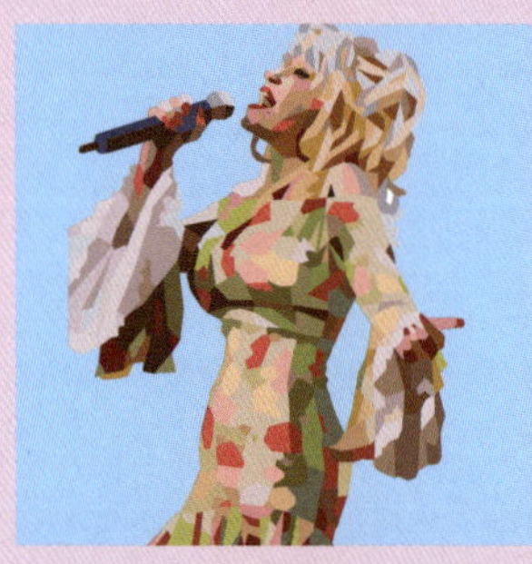
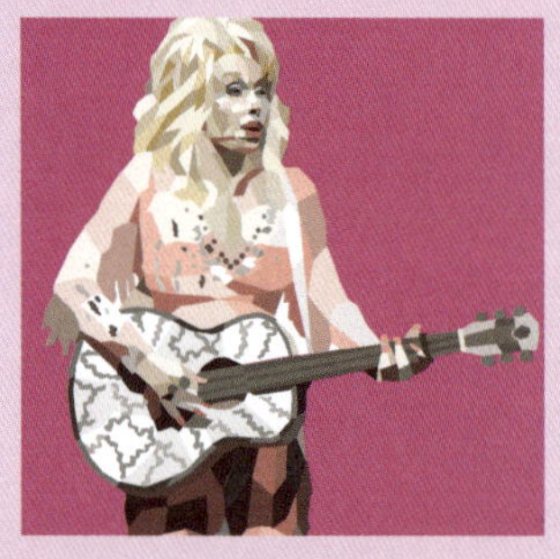
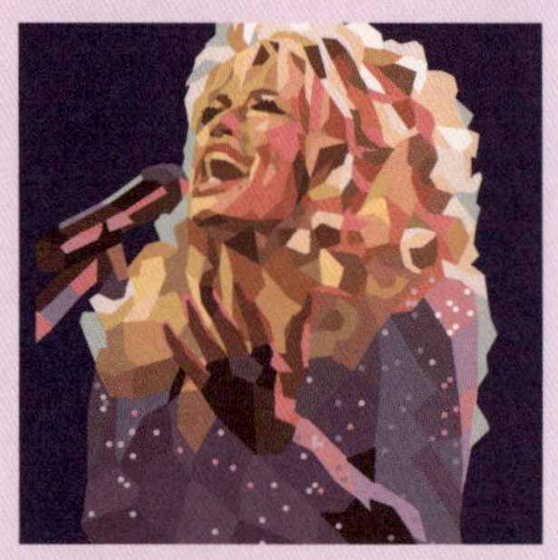
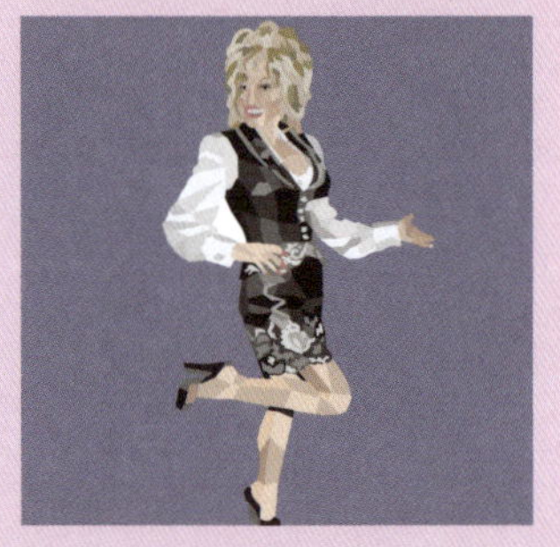
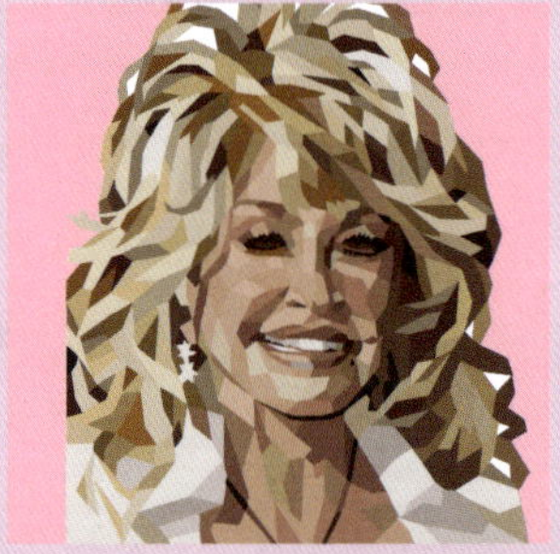
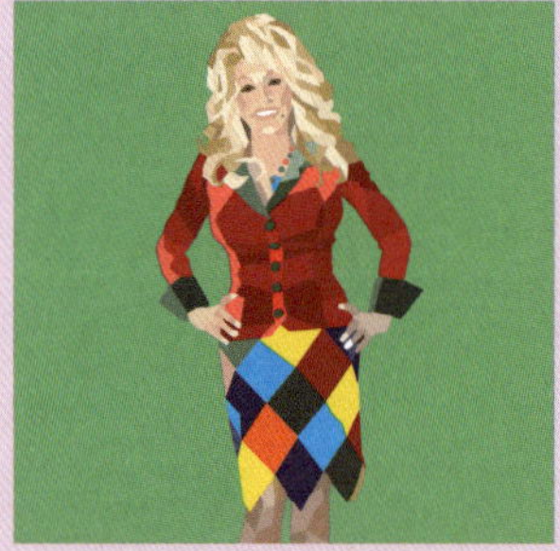
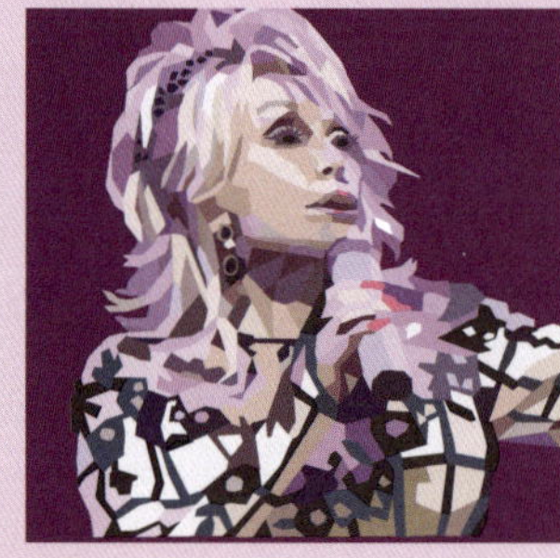
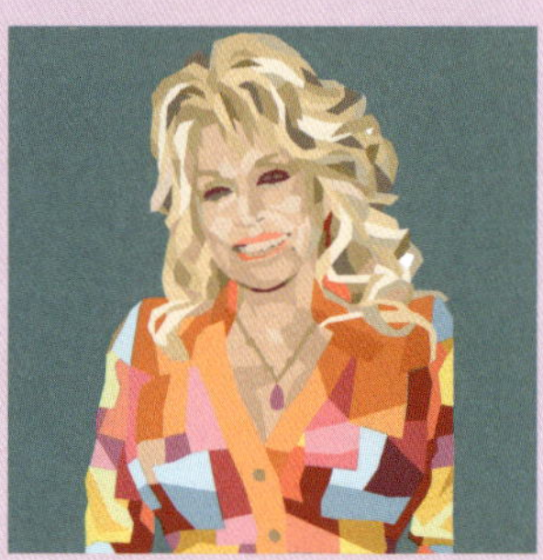
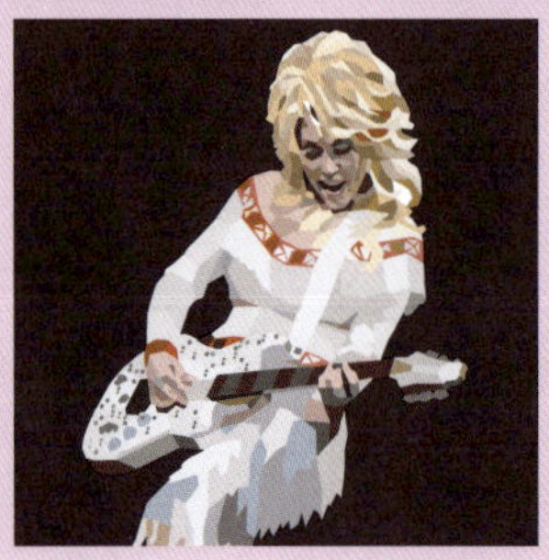
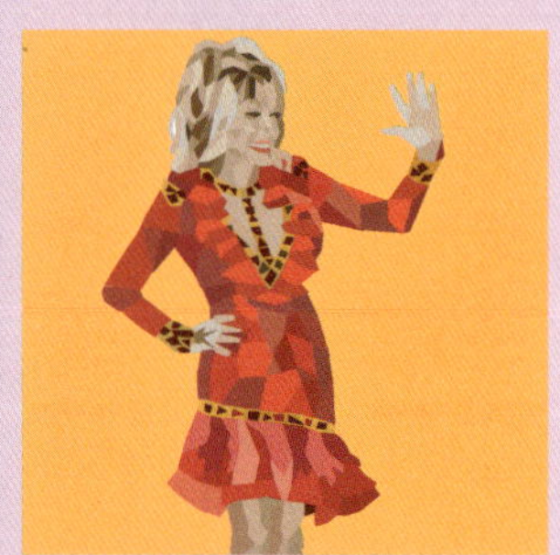

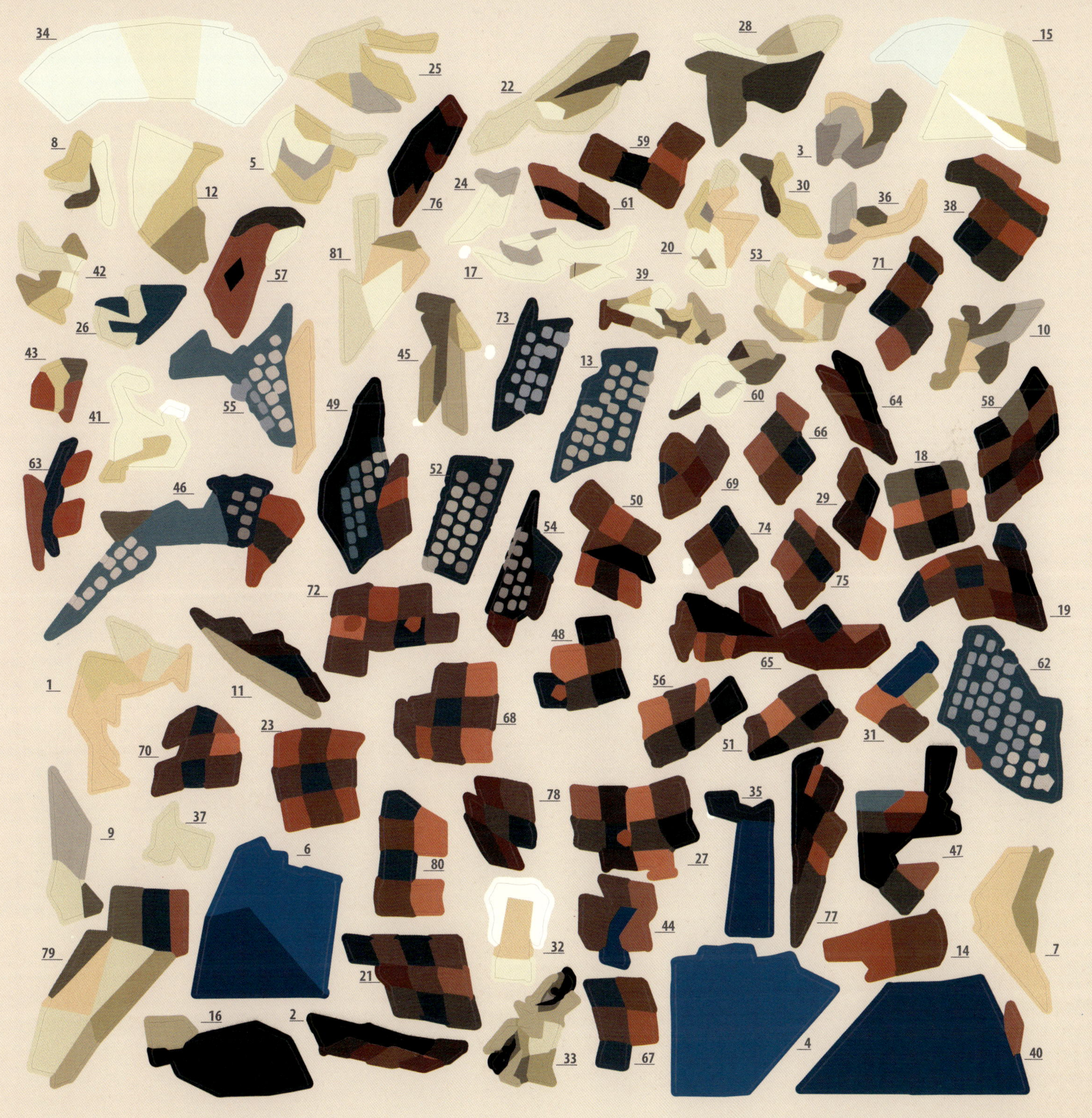

DOLLY PARTON

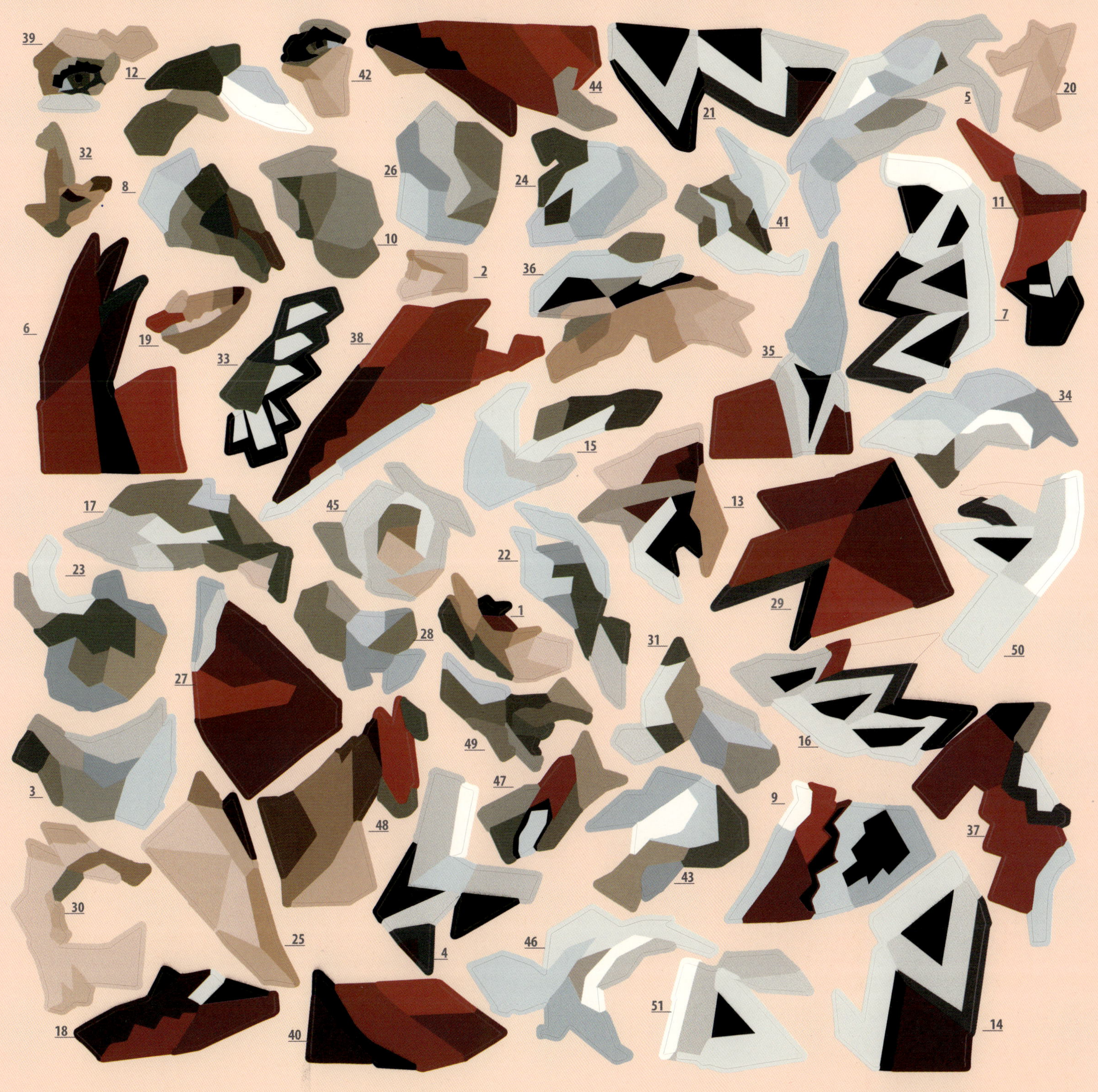

39
12
42
44
21
5
20
32
8
26
24
41
11
10
2
36
7
6
19
33
38
35
34
15
17
45
13
22
29
50
23
1
28
31
27
16
49
3
47
9
37
48
43
30
4
25
46
51
14
18
40

RISING STAR

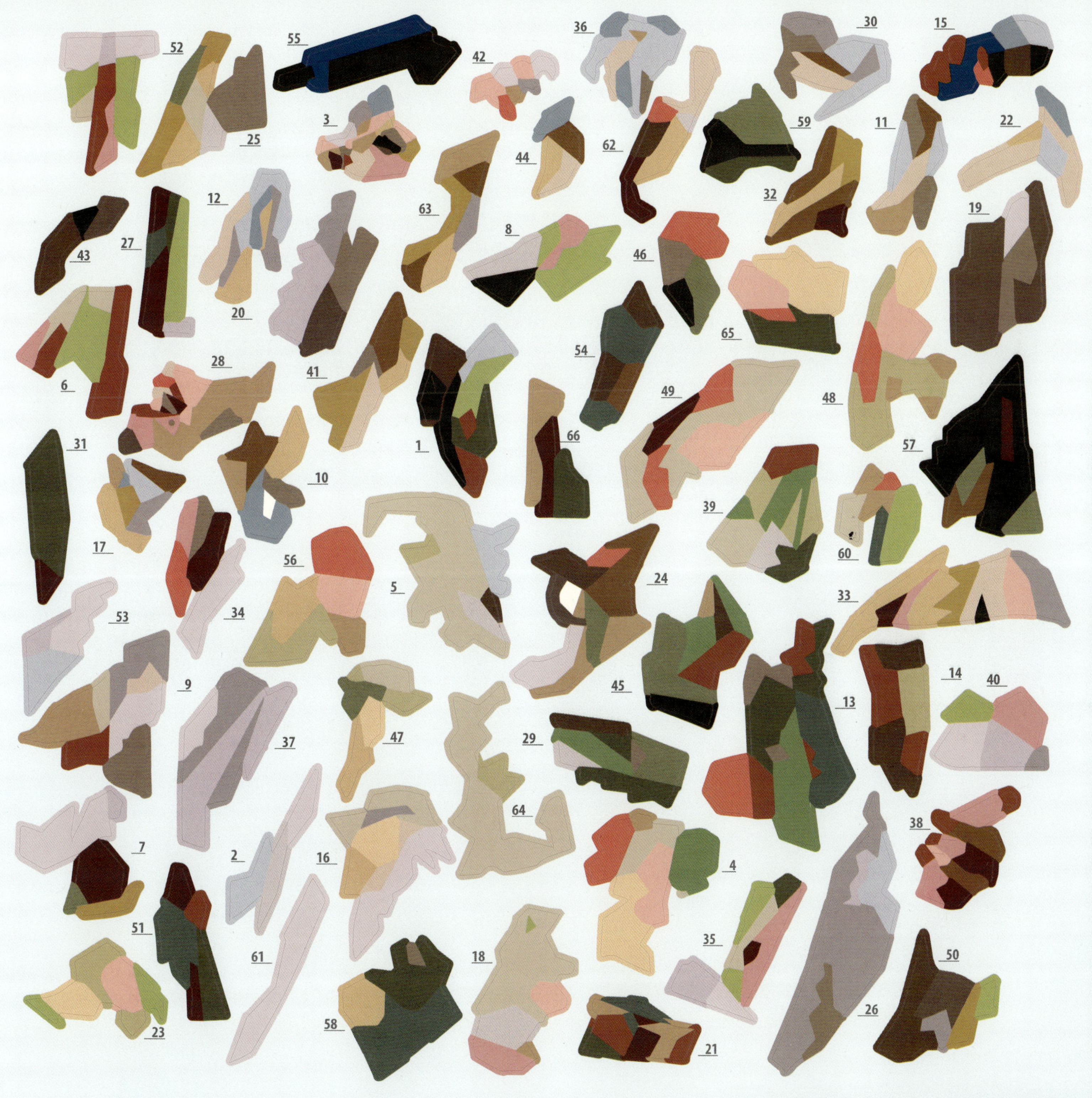

MUSICAL LEGACY

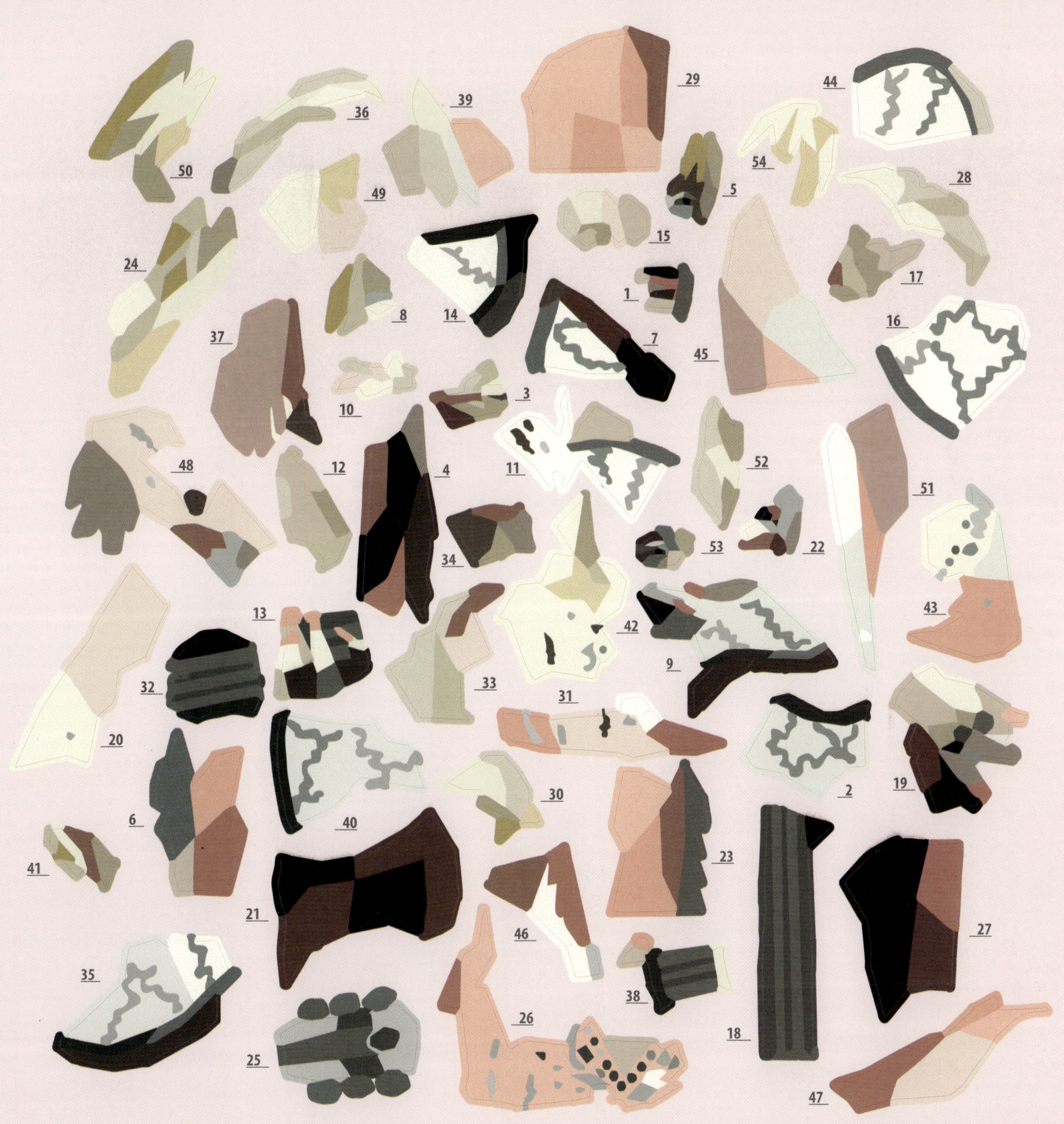

29
44
39
36
50
54
5
28
49
15
24
1
17
8
14
7
16
37
45
3
10
48
12
4
11
52
51
34
53
22
13
42
43
9
32
33
31
20
2
19
30
6
40
41
23
21
27
46
35
38
26
18
25
47

"JOLENE"

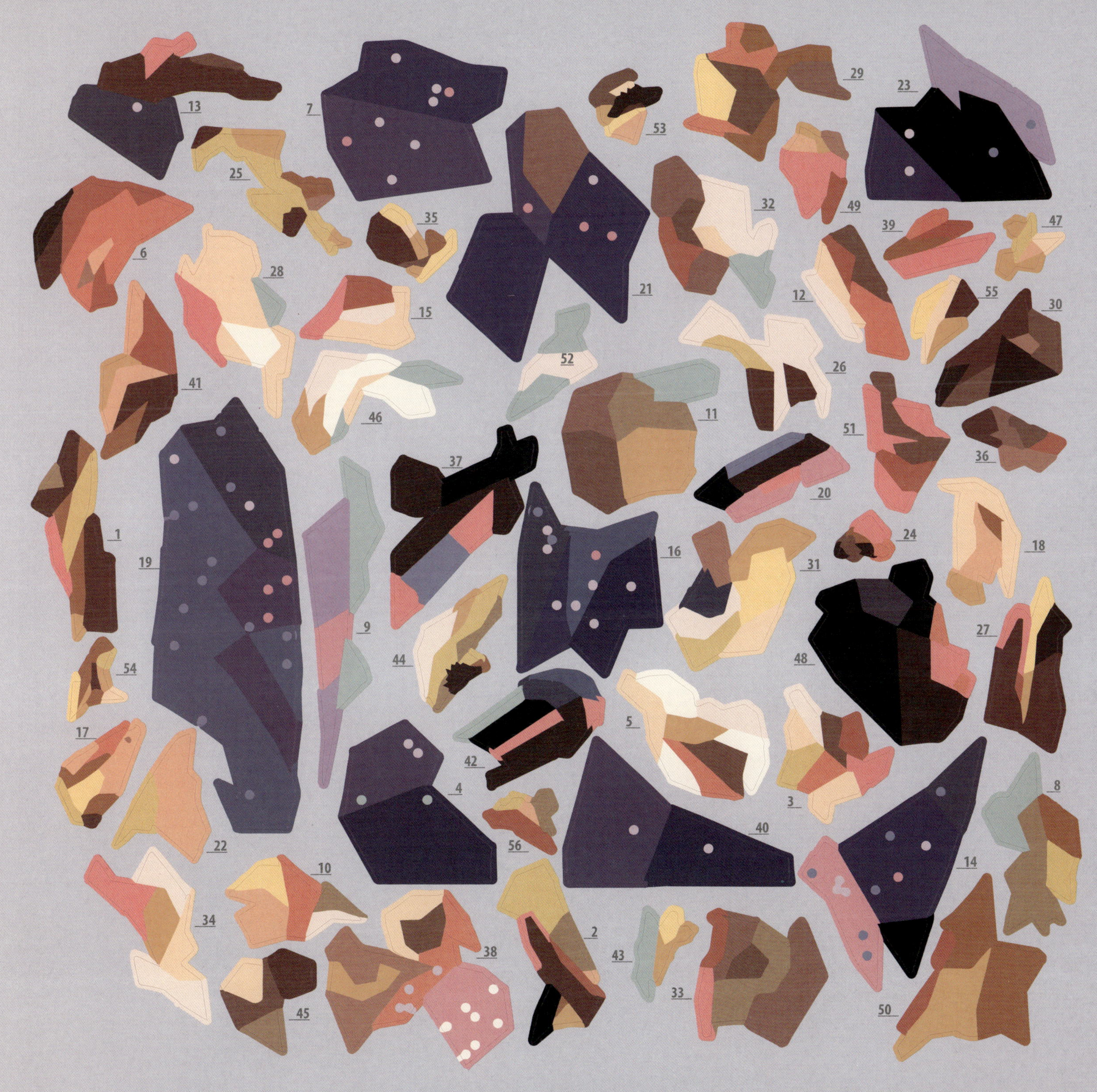

"I WILL ALWAYS LOVE YOU"

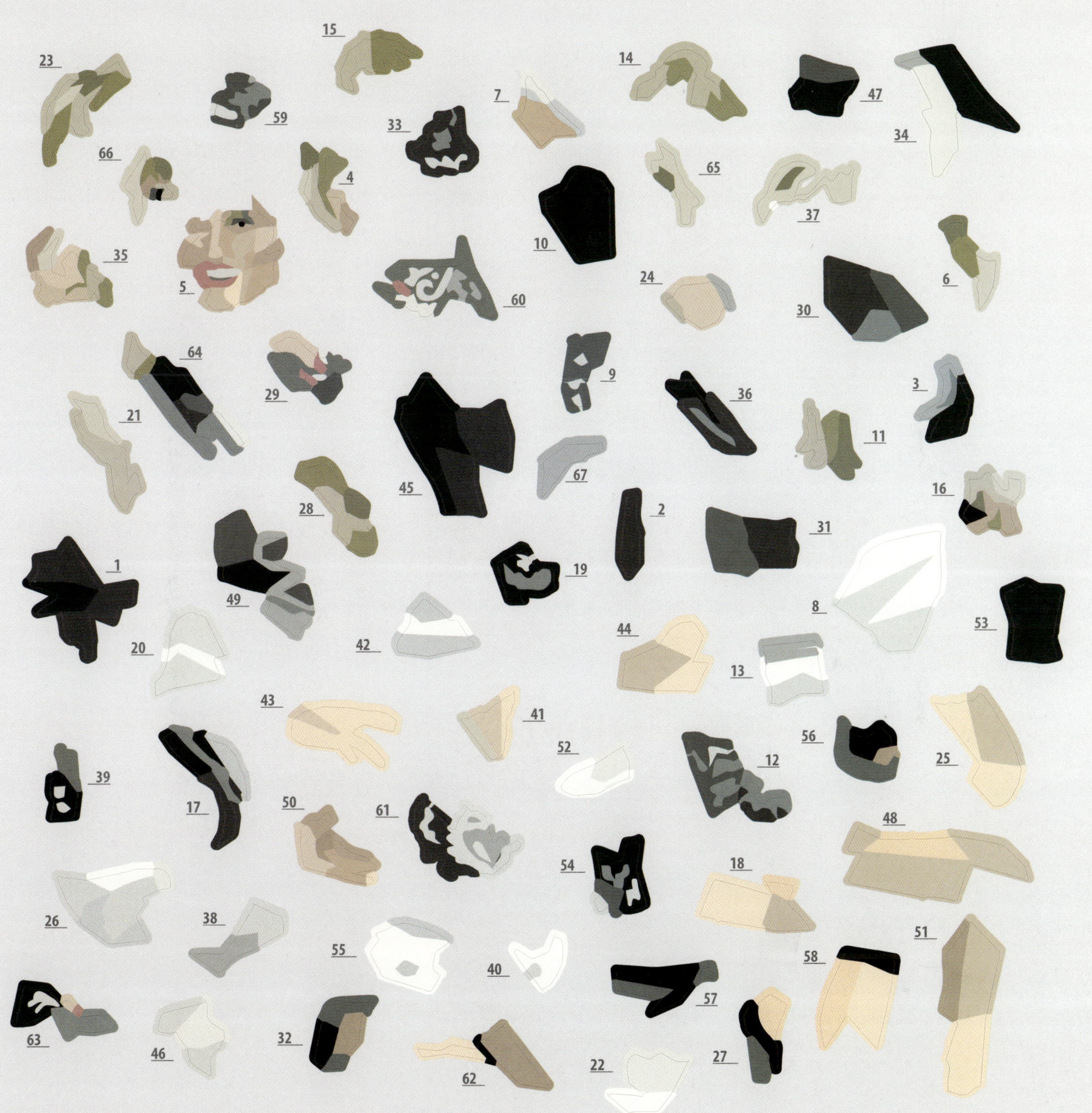

ACTING CAREER

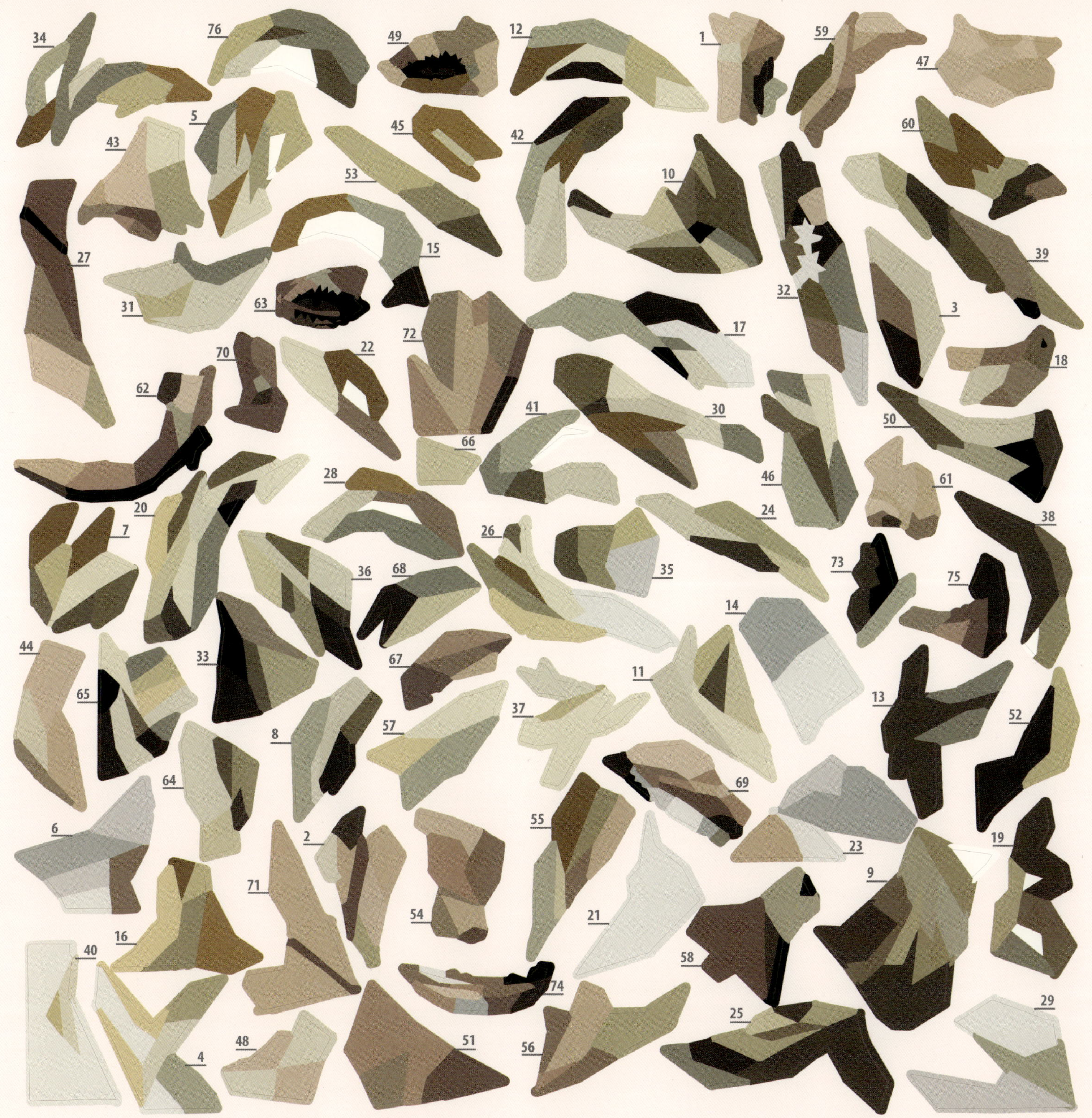

9 TO 5

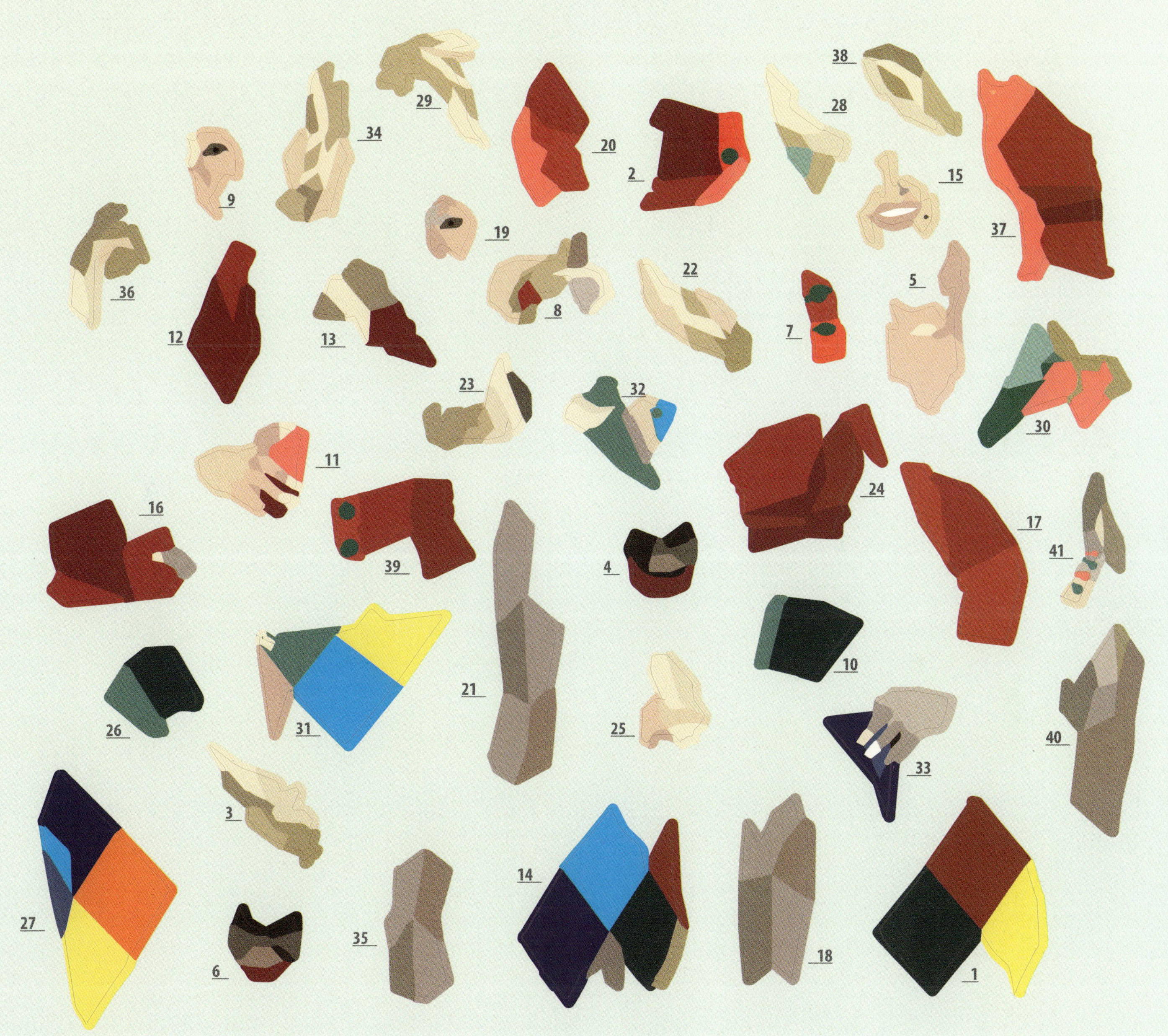

STEEL MAGNOLIAS

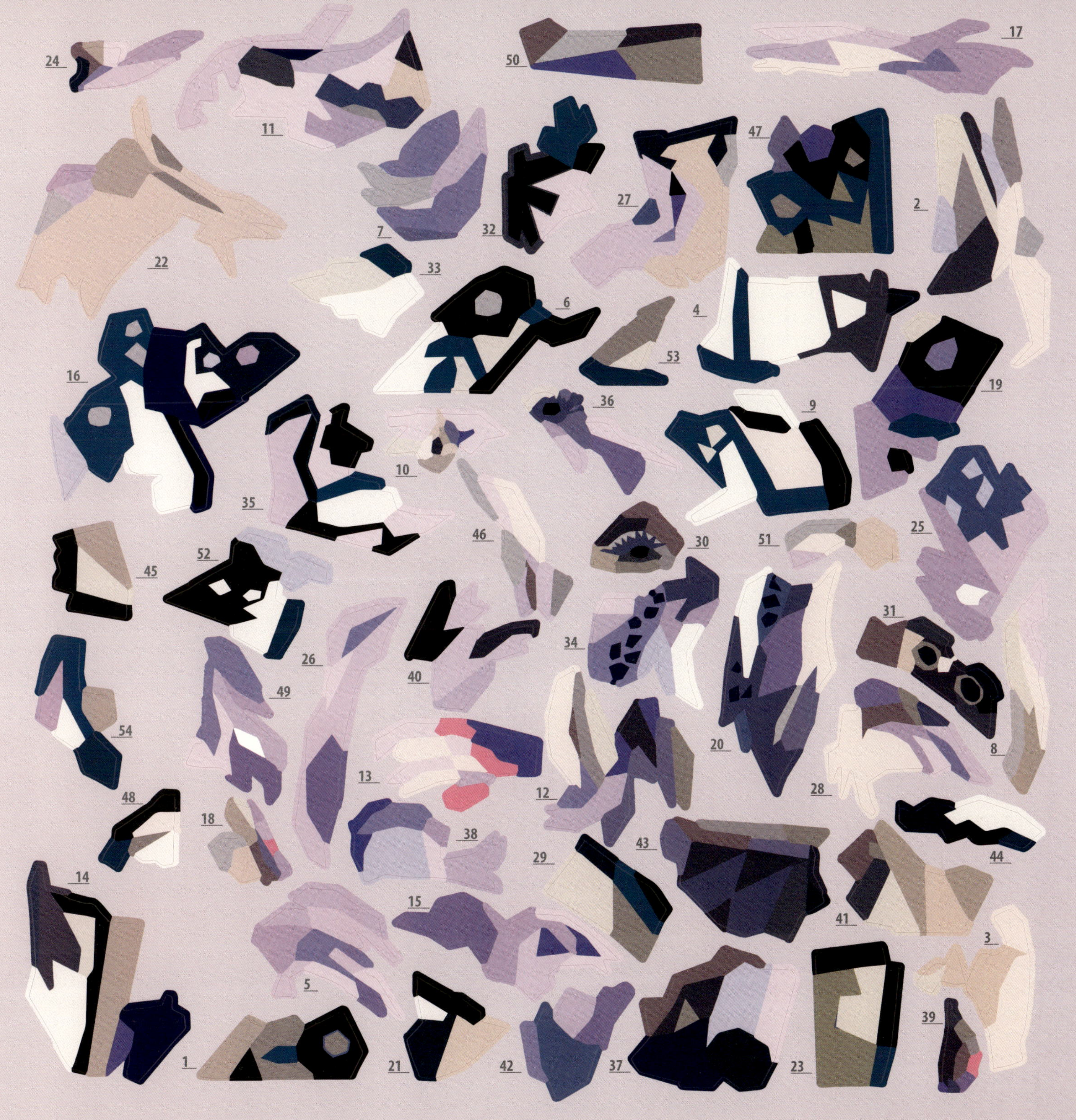

GOOD DEEDS

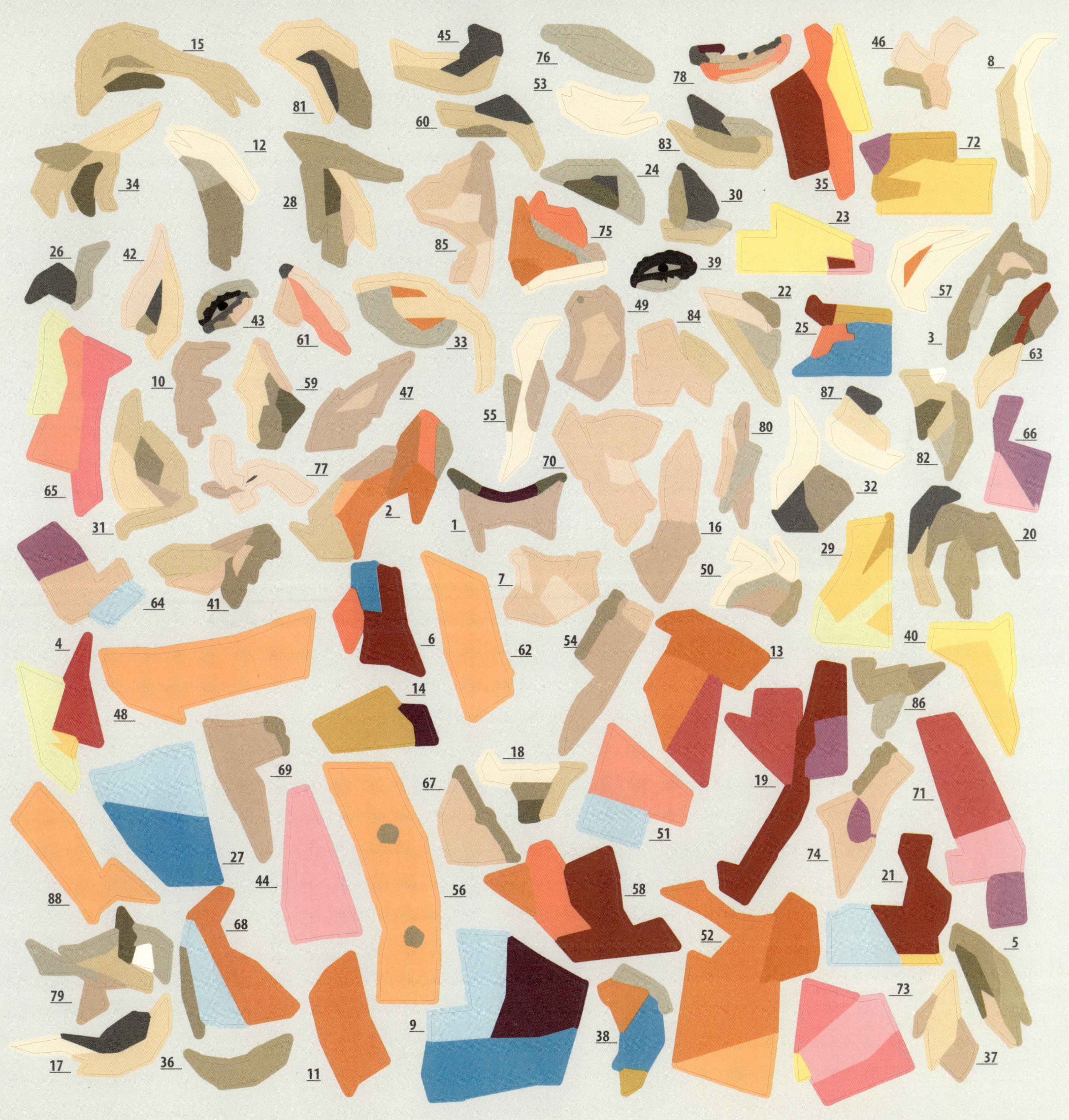
15
45
76
46
8
81
53
78
60
83
12
72
34
28
24
30
35
23
75
85
26
42
39
43
61
33
49
22
84
57
25
3
63
10
59
47
87
55
80
66
77
70
65
82
32
2
1
16
31
20
29
7
50
64
41
6
62
54
13
40
4
48
14
86
18
69
67
19
71
51
27
44
88
56
74
21
58
68
52
5
73
79
9
38
37
17
36
11

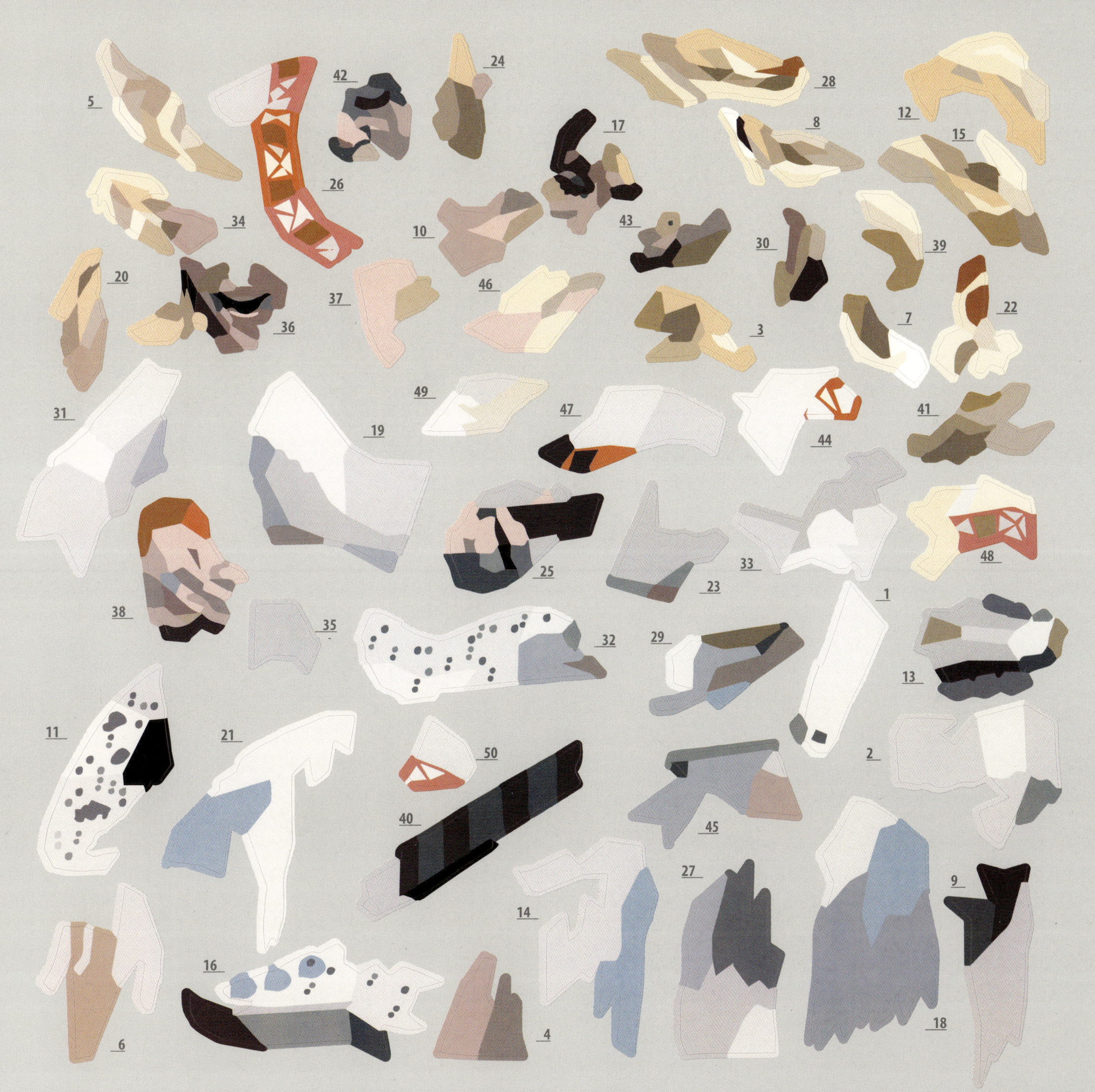

IMAGINATION LIBRARY®

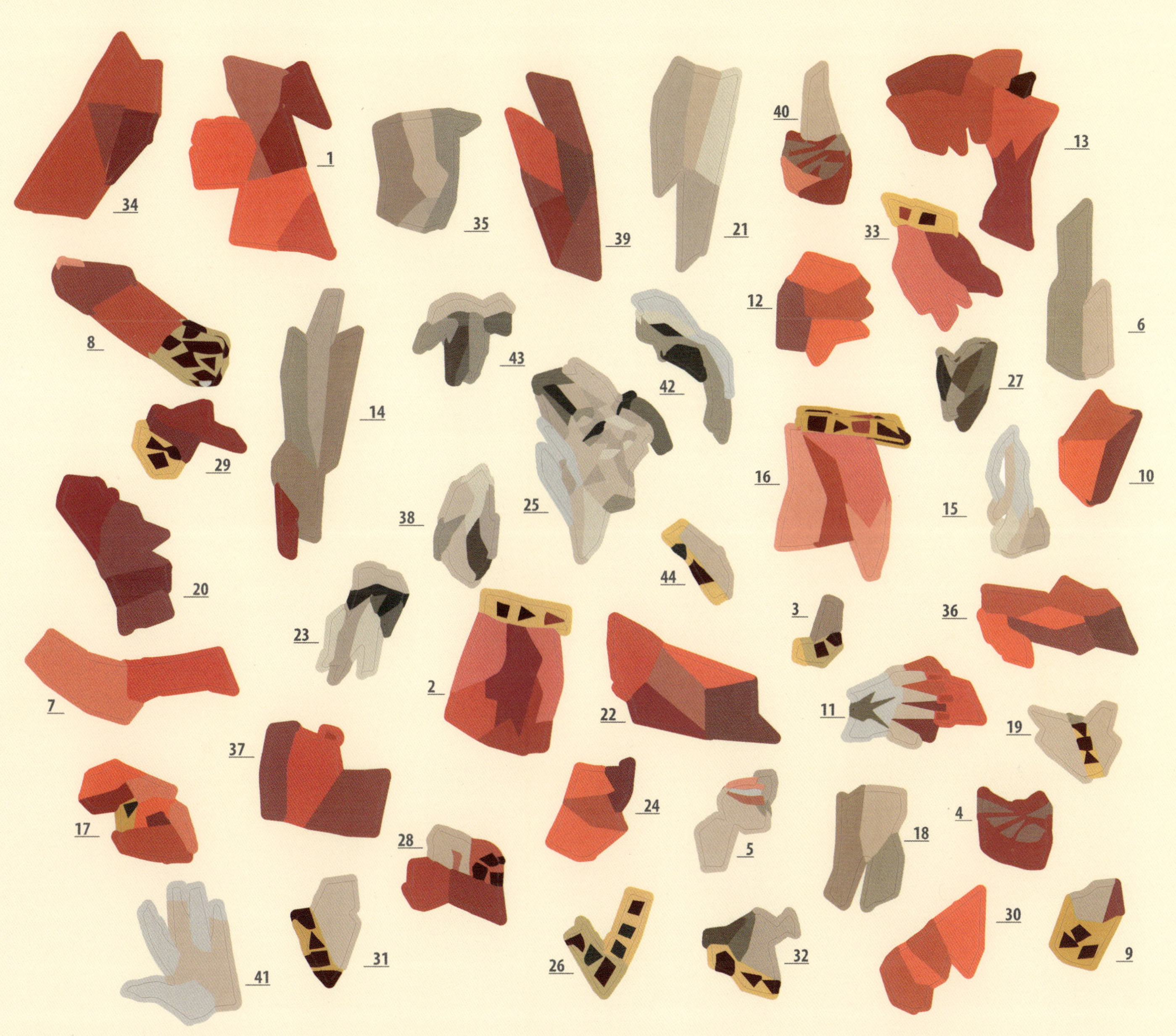

AN INSPIRATION TO ALL